Agrarian Reform in Ethiopia

Agrarian Reform in Ethiopia

Dessalegn Rahmato

Scandinavian Institute of African Studies
Uppsala, 1984

Dessalegn Rahmato is a Research Associate at the Institute of Development Research, Addis Ababa University.

For information about the Institute's research activities and publications, write to:

Institute of Development Research
Addis Ababa University
P.O. Box 1176
Addis Ababa, Ethiopia.

ISBN 91-7106-226-2
Printed in Sweden by
Motala Grafiska AB, Motala 1984

Publisher's Preface

This book is the first full-length study of the land reform and the resultant social changes in rural Ethiopia. The author, Dessalegn Rahmato, a research fellow at the Institute of Development Research, Addis Ababa University, conducted the study as part of his own wider research on the problem of transition in agrarian societies. Dessalegn spent three months in 1982 as a guest researcher at the Scandinavian Institute of African Studies (SIAS) during which time he wrote part of the draft of the manuscript. The final draft was written in Addis Ababa during the spring of 1983. SIAS is happy to publish this important study which will contribute to the understanding of the process of change taking place in rural Ethiopia.

Michael Ståhl
Director
SIAS

Contents

Acknowledgements

I wish to express my gratitude to officials of the Ministry of Agriculture in the areas of our study, to local administrative staff and rural development agents and, above all, to the many peasants and peasants leaders without whose assistance and patient co-operation this work would not have been completed.

Part of this study was written in Sweden and England. I would like to thank the Scandinavian Institute of African Studies for enabling me to spend three months in Uppsala (Sweden), and UNESCO, for another three-month stay at the Institute of Development Studies, Brighton, England.

October 1983
Dessalegn Rahmato

Short Glossary of Ethiopian Terms

Awraja, Woreda For administrative purposes the country is divided into 14 provinces. Each province is further divided into *awrajas*, and each awraja into *woredas*. The woreda is the lowest administrative unit, and the one closest to the rural community.

Chiqa-shum An official, usually resident in the rural community, who served as the administrative link between the community and the state in the old system of local government. In some communities in the south this role was carried out by the *Qoro*.

Ensat False banana plant. A long-maturing root plant which provides the staple food of the population in south-central Ethiopia.

Gasha A unit of local measurement; one Gasha is approximately 40 hectares.

Kebbelle The lowest level or unit of urban and rural organizations. The kebbelle Peasant Association is the primary organization of the peasantry.

Negarit Gazeta The official gazette where all legislation is published.

Province We have used this term rather than the recently adopted substitute, Administrative Region, for convenience and to avoid confusion. The latter term, besides being rather cumbersome, does not quite convey the meaning of the Amharic *Kifle-Hagger* which is the term technically more appropriate.

Teff A domestic cereal and the staple crop of the population in northern Ethiopia.

Woreda See Awraja.

Zematcha participants Students and teachers (about 50 thousand in all) who were sent to the countryside and the urban areas to 'organize and politicize the masses' in 1975 and 1976.

Currency

Birr At the official exchange rate, 2.07 Birr is equal to 1.00 U.S. dollar.

Chapter 1

Introduction

The Study

In content and implementation, Ethiopia's agrarian reform can be considered as a thorough and radical one. It accomplished its purpose, namely the elimination of landlordism, quite speedily—a remarkable achievement considering that at the time the reform was promulgated the new government had not yet firmly established its presence in the countryside.

The reform is undoubtedly the most important and the most far-reaching social measure of the Provisional Military Government of Ethiopia, and its impact on the fabric of rural society is far more profound than any of the reforms carried out since the overthrow of absolute monarchy. In brief, it provides for the distribution of land to peasant households, and abolishes peasant dependence on the landlord, along with the landlord himself. All rural land is under 'public ownership', and tenancy and the hiring of labour have been done away with. Since 1979, the government has called on peasants to engage in collective forms of production, but it will be a while before this policy will bear fruit, and in the meantime, independent peasant production will constitute the backbone of the country's rural economy.

We shall not attempt in the essay to present a comprehensive analysis of Ethiopia's agrarian reform, but rather will consider briefly the process of land distribution and the land system that has evolved as a result. The sections that follow will consist of:

(a) A brief look at the agrarian structure under the old regime. We shall argue that the standard approach to the analysis of the old agrarian system is inadequate and needs to be reconsidered.

(b) A summary of the content of the reform legislation

(c) A discussion of the process of land distribution and its outcome, and the evolution of Peasant Associations.

(d) Some issues on agrarian reform based on the Marxist classics.

The Ethiopian rural setting contains a wide variety of ecological zones or agro-ecological regions, of agricultural systems and practices as well as socio-cultural experiences.[1]

---

[1]For a discussion of the diversity of ecological zones and agricultural systems in Ethiopia see E. Westphal, *Agricultural Systems in Ethiopia* (Wageningen: CAPD, 1975). Also, FAO, *Agriculture in Ethiopia* (Rome: FAO, 1961; compiled by H.P. Huffnagel). Westphal has identified 11 agro-ecological regions and 4 agricultural systems in the country (pp. 81–173).

Obviously the impact of the land reform has not been uniform throughout, and in each region significant variations in substance as well as in detail have emerged.

The material for this study was collected in four select *woredas* or sub-districts located in three of the major agricultural zones of the country.* Apart from their location, the areas selected for the study reveal significant differences in terms of agricultural practices, demographic characteristics and cultural experiences. In addition, each of the woredas forms a part of a more or less distinct socio-cultural region, and each region has had a separate local history and rural economy prior to the overthrow of the *ancient regime*. The system of land holdings and the politico-administrative status of each of the regions were dis-similar enough in the past to give each area a distinctive local identity.

The tables and figures shown in the text reveal, of course, conditions in the localities where the data was collected; however, we believe that insofar as the agrarian processes and socioeconomic forces set in motion by the reform are concerned, our findings are of wider scope and relevance.

The areas of our study are the following:

1. Bollosa woreda, Wollaita awraja, Sidamo province in Southern Ethiopia.

2. Manna woreda, Jimma awraja, Kaffa province, in South-Western Ethiopia.

3. Yilmana Densa woreda (hereafter cited as Adet woreda), Bahr Dar awraja, Gojjam province in Northern Ethiopia.

4. Sibu Sire woreda (herafter Sire), Nekempte awraja, Wollega province, Central-Western Ethiopia.

Our findings are for the most part based on data gathered by means of questionnaires, personal observation, and information obtained through interviews and discussions with peasants and peasant leaders, rural development agents, and administrative officials in each of the woredas. In addition, we have also made use of records from woreda archives and documents available at local offices of Peasant Associations and rural development agencies, as well as published official and semi-official sources.

A comprehensive evaluation of the impact and consequences of the land reform on rural Ethiopia as a whole has yet to be made and in the meantime we hope this short study will serve to fill a gap.[2]

The Research Areas

Bollosa. The Wollaita region, in which Bolloso is located, and of which the latter is one of the most productive woredas, falls within what is known as the zone of

---

*The meanings of Ethiopian terms frequently used in this work are given in the Glossary.

[2]For some initial assessments of the reform see: Bruce; Cohen et al. (1977 and 1976); Goricke; Hoben (1976); M. Ottaway; and Ståhl (1977). All are basically first impressions, and contain no serious research; many in fact confine themselves to comments on the reform legislation.

ensat culture. This agro-ecological zone extends over a wide area in south-central Ethiopia, and includes the areas of the Gurage, Kambatta-Hadiya, and part of the provinces of Sidamo, Gamo Goffa and Kaffa. It is estimated that over 6 million people depend on ensat for their staple food, and more importantly, the inhabitants in the region share many things in common, in particular agricultural practices and technique, patterns of settlement, etc. Bollosa is among the better-off of Wollaita's woredas, and the beneficiary of many years of infrastructural and extension work by the Wollaita Agricultural Development Unit (WADU), a rural development agency based in Wollaita-Soddo, the awraja capital.

In addition to the staple crop, ensat, peasants in Bollosa grew a wide variety of cereals, vegetables and fruit. The most common cereals are maize, teff, barley and sorghum, while root crops such as yam, taro, sweet and irish potatoes are important supplements of peasant diet. In the drier parts of the woreda, cash crops such as coffee, ginger and cotton are raised. Farm plots here are of miniscule size—the average being about 0.25 ha—and each plot is divided into a number of subplots for the purpose of multiple cropping. Peasants do not, as a general rule, choose to rely on one or two crops however tiny their plots may be, instead they prefer to minimise the risks of failure and food shortage by cultivating a large number of crops and vegetables. This pattern of holding and form of cultivation is typical not only of Wollaita peasants but those in the ensat zone as well.

Although, or perhaps because, farm plots are small and land is an extremely scarce commodity, the intense and relatively better methods of cultivation used by peasants in Bolloso has enabled the area to avoid the kind of food crisis that has affected many regions in the country. The average Bolloso peasant uses a greater amount of natural fertiliser (manure) on his plots, gives more time and attention to his crops, and in general looks after his farm with much greater care and skill than his counterpart in the three woredas in our study.

As is typical in all of Wollaita, or indeed in the agricultural zone in which the region is located, farm techniques in Bolloso combine the use of ox power with that of hand tools, especially hoes. Ox ploughing is not indigenous to the area, having been introduced from elsewhere at some time in the past. However, the plough and hoe cultures now complement each other so that hand tools are still as important though not as valuable as oxen and ploughs. According to a WADU study of 1976, 58% of the population in the area used oxen for cultivation, and 42% hand hoes.[3]

Previous to the land reform, the majority of Bolloso peasants were small owner cultivators, and tenancy was not very widespread. Those who were considered large holders were those who owned over 5 hectares of land, some of which they rented out to tenant cultivators, but this group formed a small percentage of the rural population. Landlords not indigenous to the area—that is, outsiders and absentee owners—were not a significant force in Bolloso.

---

[3] *1976 General Agricultural Survey* Report, WADU Pub. No. 58, Wollaita-Soddo, 1976, p. 19.

Thanks to WADU's road building efforts, the woreda is served by a large *network* of rural access roads, and in this Bolloso is unique among all of the country's rural communities. Each of the 43 Peasant Association offices scattered throughout the district, and indeed, a large majority of individual peasant homes, can be reached by cross-country vehicles and small to medium trucks. The main purpose of these roads that criss-cross the countryside, and make Bolloso the most accessible rural community in the country, was to open up the area for agricultural support services, to encourage the process of integration of the rural community and to expand the volume of exchange between town and country. It is doubtful whether the purpose has been achieved; indeed, it seems evident that the wider communication network has had no significant impact on the economic life of the community.

WADU's efforts have not been restricted to road building alone, it has been active in providing general extension services in the area for over a decade. Here again, the result of rural development effort—and the three other areas in our study have not been the beneficiaries of this kind of attention—is not readily apparent, and Bolloso peasants are in the main no different in their attitude to new techniques and improved methods of cultivation from those elsewhere.

With a rural population of about 100,000, and an area far smaller than any of our woredas, Bolloso is the most densely populated area in our study. The population, made up almost exclusively of Wollaita-speaking people, is culturally homogeneous, although religious and clan distinctions exist and often play a part in the life of the rural community. A small but active minority, made up of Protestant and Catholic converts, has over the years managed to establish a sub-culture and a social importance within traditional Wollaita society.

Unlike Adet or Sire, where rural settlements are widely scattered, peasant homesteads here are contiguous to one another, and the family plot forms an extension of the homestead. Each peasant home looks like an island surrounded by a sea of green ensat plants, coffee and fruit trees, vegetables, and seasonal crops.

The whole countryside is densely settled and made up of a string of small hamlets and 'baby' plots—the closest thing to village forms of settlement in Ethiopia.

In contrast to many woredas in the country, Bolloso has always been self-sufficient in food crops, and in times of good harvest produces a surplus in teff, maize and barley. This may be partly due to the fact that the standard diet of the rural population consists for the most part of root crops and vegetables, and the peasantry grows cereals, particularly teff and maize, as cash crops. Areka, the woreda capital and the main trading centre for the people in the area, is a busy town on market days, attracting peasant traders, grain merchants and small business-men from as far as Hossana, some 80 kms away.

Manna. Our second district is in the heart of the coffee growing region of Kaffa province, the woreda itself being the biggest producer of coffee in Jimma awraja. Here too, the area is relatively well endowed in terms of transport and communication facilities, and a number of dry-weather roads provide adequate access to the rural areas. Coffee is the main crop here, but other side-line products include maize, teff, barley, chat and fruit. The traditional form of coffee cultivation involves virtually no implements, and the average peasant in Manna owns only a hand hoe and a 'Gedjera'—a long-bladed metal tool, somewhat like a machete, used for stripping trees and clearing underbrush. Both here and in Bolloso, the livestock population is very small and, as we shall see in the main text of our discussion, a large number of peasants possess few or no work-stock or cattle.

With a rural population of about 130,000, and a relatively large land area, Manna is densely populated and fairly big for a woreda. The pattern of habitation resembles that of Bolloso, although it is not as dense and close-knit as the latter, and again land here is very scarce. The population is predominantly Moslem, and polygamy—which became a source of conflict during land distribution—is widely practiced. It may be noted in passing that multiple marriages in Ethiopia are not restricted to Moslem areas; the practice exists in many non-Moslem communities such as for instance Wollaita. Manna is the least ethnically homogeneous of our woredas, with about 78% of the rural population Oromo and the rest of different cultural stock.

The woreda has always been a grain-deficit area, 'importing' much of its food from other regions. It has periodically experienced severe food shortages, and on the eve of the land reform, a government report forecast that the area was about to face one of its worst food crises in many decades.[4] This is partly due to the fact that a large portion of the agricultural land—about 45% of it—is under coffee, and food-grain cultivation suffers from the general poverty of the peasantry and their lack of adequate work stock, implements and land for cereal cultivation.

Although plough cultivation is widespread, and the peasant with a pair of farm oxen and a plough is considered fortunate and fairly 'prosperous', hoe cultivation is also quite common. The peasant here divides his holding into two plots, one for coffee trees and another for growing food crops, and the latter is often a small plot, frequently a backyard garden, which is worked by hand tools and quite often by women and the younger members of the family. It is worth noting that both here and in Bolloso—and in contrast to Adet and Sire—the poorer members of the peasantry rely on the cultivation, and the growing of root crops, vegetables and the like for their basic needs. Prior to the land reform a large portion of Manna peasants were involved in tenancy, and a majority of holdings were below 0.5 ha in size. The landowning classes were predominantly outsiders, and absentee owners greatly outnumbered local resident owners.

Adet in Gojjam, and Sire in Wollega. We shall deal with these two areas together because both are basically within the same agro-ecological zone. They are predominantly areas of cereal production. One reason for our choice of these

---

[4]See Ministry of Agriculture, *Report of the Crop Condition Survey*, Addis Ababa, Ministry of Agriculture, 1974.

two woredas, however, was because we felt that each in its own way represents rural conditions, both before and after the reform, of northern and western Ethiopia, respectively.

Farm technique and cultivation methods are identical in both areas––peasants rely exclusively on ox power for cultivation. As far as agricultural practice and general rural conditions are concerned, a peasant from Adet would be quite at home in Sire and vice versa. The same cannot be said of the Bolloso or Manna peasant, any one of whom would be in serious difficulty outside of his specific agro-cultural environment. The similarity of Adet and Sire also extends to the pattern of rural settlement where homesteads are scattered over a large area and farm plots usually some distance away from peasant dwellings. This form of habitation is characteristic of most cereal growing regions of highland Ethiopia.

In terms of basic infrastructure, the areas are among the most severely deprived in the country, and a great portion of the rural community in both localities is virtually inaccessible. The two woredas are fairly large in physical size, but while Adet with a rural population of 120,000 is among the larger of our research areas, Sire with 55,000 inhabitants is among the least populated woredas in the country. According to a government survey, both areas are considered to be grain surplus areas; however, during periods of poor harvest both equally face crisis of food shortage for the reason that peasants in neither case are strong enough to support themselves by grain purchases, or have alternative sources of food.[5] In a sense, peasants in Adet and Sire are far more insecure than their counterparts in Bolloso or Manna and, paradoxical though it may seem, this is in part a consequence of the plough culture which, on the other hand, is considered to be superior to the hoe culture.

Prior to the land reform, Adet and Sire fell within the two prevalent tenure systems of the country. While the former was part of what was known as the *rist* (or communal) system, discussed at some length in Section 2 of this essay, the latter was predominantly a tenancy area. Both our own findings and official studies show that a large majority of peasants in Sire were tenants under the old land system. Characteristically, large landowners were a significant force here, but the landowners consisted of 'outsiders' as well as indigenous elements.

The population of both woredas is culturally homogeneous, and forms of cleavage along ethnic, religious or clan lines do not exist, or are of minor significance. In Adet, the peasantry is overwhelmingly Amhara, and in Sire, Oromo. On average, peasant holdings in Adet, both before and after the reform, are larger in size than in any of our other woredas, and in both cases the intensity of land hunger was far less than either in Bolloso or Manna.

The Scope of the Study

The fieldwork for the study was begun in September 1980 and completed about

---

[5]Ibid.

seven months later, in March 1981. In order to make our coverage as wide as possible, we used a fairly large sample of peasant households for our questionnaires. Our sample was based on a selection of 20% of the Peasant Associations (PAs) in each woreda, and a random selection of 10% of the registered members of each Peasant Association. The number of PAs in any locality is not fixed or stable; it changes periodically as boundaries within PAs as well as within localities are redrawn, land is freshly redistributed, etc. Each PA has a record—not always very accurate or up to date, unfortunately—of its members who are holders of land *on behalf of* their households.

The number of PAs and household heads selected for our questionnaires is shown in the Table 1.

Table 1. *Number of Peasant Associations and Household Heads Selected for the Survey*

	Total no. of PAs	No. of PAs selected	No. of Household heads selected
Bolloso	43	9	531
Manna	48	10	735
Adet	52	10	524
Sire	45	9	188
Total	188	38	1978

Except in Sire, the average membership in each PA in our woredas is considerably high, much higher than the national average which is about 200. As can be seen from the table, we administered close to 2000 questionnaires.

Our study is concerned exclusively with the private sector of rural production, and we have not attempted to deal with rural cooperatives or the process of cooperativisation. This is because the Government's cooperatives programme had just been launched, but was not being seriously or actively implemented, when we were doing our field work.

Chapter 2

The Agrarian System under the Old Regime

Introduction

No thorough and conclusive study has yet been made of the agrarian system of the old regime, and this may be both because of the paucity of reliable data, and because of the complex and confusing tenurial structure that existed in the country before the land reform.

In this section, we shall not attempt a detailed analysis, but will present only a brief sketch, focusing on the salient features of the system. Thus particular attention will be focussed on the tenurial arrangement that prevailed, the pattern of holdings, the distribution of rights of access to land, and the relationship between the direct producers and their overlords. Any discussion of these and related questions is of course a hazardous undertaking since the empirical evidence is either unavailable, partial or of questionable quality. Nevertheless, some conclusions can be made on the basis of what *is* available. Our discussion in this section therefore relies on the findings of official studies conducted by the Ministry of Land Reform (MLR), which is now defunct, the Ministry of Agriculture, and the Central Statistical Office (CSO).[1]

It has often been argued that the old agrarian system can best be described as feudal. The relation between those who controlled the sources of rural wealth and those who produced it, and the social status of the latter in the overall political economy of the country, were essentially feudal in nature, and the Ethiopian feudalism concept provides the most useful framework for an analysis of rural production.[2] This approach is valid to a certain extent, but it should be recognised that it does not fully explain *all* the intricacies of the land system in *all* parts of the country. Certainly, feudal relations of production existed in substantial portions of the country, in particular in the southern and south-

---

[1]Much of the data in the literature on the land question is based on these studies. Some of the main secondary sources on the subject are: J.M. Cohen and D. Weintraub: *Land and Peasants in Imperial Ethiopia* (Assen: Van Gorcum, 1975); P. Gilkes: *The Dying Lion* (London: J.Friedmann, 1973); John Markakis: *Ethiopia, Anatomy of a Traditional Policy* (Oxford Clarendon Press, 1974), especially Chapters 4 and 5); H.S. Mann: *Land Tenure in Ghora (Shoa)* (Addis Ababa, 1965).

[2]Cohen and Weintrabu strongly argue in favour of this position, see pp. 11−20.

western regions. However, the 'tributary' systems of the northern areas cannot be adequately explained within the framework of Ethiopian feudalism. Moreover, a close and detailed examination will reveal that even in the south, Ethiopian feudalism had a hybrid content, containing elements from a number of non- or pre-feudal forms, and varying in character from one region to another.

The Landholding System

Despite the objections of some writers, it is, we believe, valid to make a distinction between the tenure systems of the north and those of the south, although, as we shall see in a moment, the geographical approach has limited explanatory value. Both in the north and south, there were a large number of landholding arrangements—perhaps as many as twenty different varieties— —and the student who attempts to examine them all may easily get bogged down in fruitless technicalities.

One can however isolate the core element of each of these tenures and show that many of them share commonalities, and can therefore be grouped together. The standard method of classification identifies four major tenures. These are: in the north, what is often termed the 'communal', church, and state tenures. Cohen and Weintraub argue that the term 'communal' is inappropriate, and that the tenure in question should instead be called the 'kinship' (and its Tigrai variant, the 'village') tenure.[3] The term perhaps most technically appropriate is *rist* tenure. In the south, the tenures were church, stade and private.

Let us now briefly discuss each of these tenures. In the communal system, an individual was said to have rights to land, or rist rights, in a given farming community if he was able to establish descent from one who was recognised to be the original holder of the land in question or the founder of the community. The extended or multiple family, or corporation in Hoben's term, holds the rights to all the land, and all those, male as well as female, who could demonstrate kinship ties to the original founder or his heirs, were entitled to a share of land.[4] The individual obtains usufruct rights over his holdings, which could not however be transferred to others by sale, mortgage or gift, although the possessor could lease them to others. His rist right was for life, and upon his death the land was divided equally among all his children, male and female. The individual with rist rights may not be a resident of the community, but his rights were honoured when he put in his claim, that is, when he gave proof that he was entitled to a share.

---

[3]All official publications, however, use the term 'communal', and this is the main reason why we shall not dispense with it in this discussion.
[4]For a more extended discussion, see Hoben, op.cit., especially Chapters 6 to 9. A short analysis of *rist* tenure is contained in his earlier work: 'Social Anthropology and Development Planning ... in Ethiopia', *Journal of Modern African Studies*, Vol. 10, No. 4, 1972.

Under this system, each member of the community was assured a piece of land, however small it was, since any 'legitimate' member's claims were always honoured. This had led some to argue that the system minimised landlessness, for, in Hoben's words, it was effective in allocating land to people and people to land. The community as a whole paid tribute to the state over all the lands under its control, each holder contributing his share in accordance with his holdings. Quite a few members of the community held additional plots in other communities on the same principle, that is, by establishing kinship ties.

Another tenurial arrangement here was known as *Gult*, which was property, usually in the form of large estates, granted to members of the ruling aristocracy. Rights to gult were granted to those who were recognised to have performed loyal service to the crown, and recipients were empowered to collect taxes or tribute from the people on gult property and to exercise administrative and judicial authority in the area. Gult estates were worked by tributary peasants, but the granting power, usually the state, held reversionary right over such estates.

The communal system, which was widely practiced in the northern provinces, notably in Gojjam, Gondar, northern Shoa, Wollo and Tigrai, has been seen by some as a flexible and accommodating one. It has been argued that in it the chances for social mobility were greater, landlessness and tenancy were minimised, and most important of all, peasants were assured security of tenure.[5] Although the empirical evidence is incomplete, what is available shows that such arguments cannot be wholly sustained. Most official studies, and our own personal investigations in Bahr Dar awraja in Gojjam province, reveal that the system gave rise to excessive fragmentation and diminution of holdings. Peasants we interviewed here were unanimous in pointing out that this was the most serious flaw of the system.

Each new claimant—and the system encouraged innumerable claims and counterclaims—demanded his share as legitimate heir to his father's and mother's rist; and his wife similarly did the same. If successful, such a peasant would have a number of plots scattered all over the community, and in others as well. In addition, each holder's plots were divided among all his children at the time of his death so that his heirs would similarly end up with mini-plots in different parts of the community.

Let us look at the case of Gojjam where, according to a survey of the Ministry of Land Reform (MLR) of 1971, 80% of the land in the province was rist land.[6] In Bahr Dan awraja, only 15% of peasants had holdings of one parcel. The number of parcels individually operated ran to as many as 8, with 59% of holders working 3 and more parcels, and 34% more than 4 parcels. The

---

[5]Allen Hoben is one advocate of this system. See both his works cited above, especially *Land Tenure* ...., pp. 226–232.

[6]The evidence for what follows comes from MLR.: *Report on Land Tenure Survey of Gojjam Province* (Addis Ababa, 1971); hereafter cited as MLR *Gojjam*. Similarly with the other MLR provincial reports.

problem of diminution of plots noted above, which was a result of the constant division and sub-division of holdings, is shown by the distribution of size of holdings in the province. According to the same survey, 54% of holdings here were less than 1 hectare in size, and only 16% above 2 hectares.

It is true that in Gojjam as well as the other communal tenure areas, tenancy was not widespread, although a small percentage of tenants did exist (13% in Gojjam, 9% in Gondar, and 7% in Tigrai)[7]; this was one of the positive sides of the system. Rist areas were far from conducive to tenancy and, due to demographic pressure, excess land was not available. Tenants were also highly insecure in their holdings for the reason that their plots could be taken away any time new claimants appeared and their demands were honoured.

The argument that the communal practice encouraged security of tenure needs to be looked at closely. In theory, rist holders acquired land for life, but quite often their rights were challenged by others who claimed the land in question on the grounds of closer ties to one or other of the ancestors in the corporate family system. This was one of the chief causes for endless conflict among peasants, where disputants spent years in unprofitable and costly ligitation, and where as a consequence the lands in question were left unused or poorly looked after. In addition, in some parts of the communal areas, periodic redistribution of communal land, to accomodate newcomers as well as to upgrade the less privileged, was not uncommon. In this case the insecurity of holders was aggravated and the incentive for proper care of their holdings minimised.

The Ethiopian coptic church was reputedly an extensive land holder both in the north as well as in the south. In truth, how much land it held will most probably never be known, although a rough estimate could be made on the basis of existing but incomplete data. One such estimate was offered by Cohen and Weintraub who suggested that up to 20% of the country's cultivated land belonged to the church[8]. We believe that this is somewhat exaggerated, and the available evidence suggests that a figure of 10 to 12% may be closer to the truth.

Church land, the most common of which has called *semon* land, was land which in theory belonged to the state but the rights of which had been granted to the church in perpetuity. Semon land was meant to be used to enable the church to support its activities, its clergy and others who provided service to it. The church as an institution did not itself carry on agricultural activity, it leased the land instead to others in return for tribute or tax. Those who operated semon holdings could in turn rent them out to others, either on a crop-sharing basis or in payment of a fixed tribute, but they could not sell, mortgage, or exchange them in other ways. They could however pass them on to their heirs provided that the recipients agreed to carry on the obligations of

---

[7]MLR: *Draft Policy of the Imperial Ethiopian Government on Agricultural Land Tenure* (Addis Ababa, 1972), mimeo, p. 8.

[8]Cited in Note 64, p. 68.

their legators, i.e. the payment of tax and the provision of service to the institution.

In effect, both the church and the holders had only usufruct rights over semon land, and in this sense semon tenures shared certain common features with communal and village tenures. The church acted in much the same way as the corporate family or village, that is, it held rights of possession over land which it then distributed to its clergy, servitors and parishioners. The difference was of course that semon holders were required to pay to the church rather than the state the required tribute or tax.

Under a variety of classifications, the most important of which were known as *maderia* and *mengist,* the state held vast tracts of agricultural land throughout the country, and especially in the southern regions. As in the case of church land, the full extent of state holdings has not been accurately determined. Some official studies indicate that the state was the dominant landholder in several areas in the south. In Nekempte awraja, Wollega province, for instance, 31% of the measured land was state owned,[9] and in Jimma awraja, Kaffa province, state holdings comprised 44% of the measured land.[10] Cohen and Weintraub have estimated that about 12% of all the agricultural land of the country was held by the state, but this, in our opinion, greatly under-estimates the size of state holdings.

Some of this land was leased out to individual cultivators, and in this way a large number of tenants were dependent on state land. A good portion of it was however given out to individuals (maderia land), or registered as government property (mengist land). The former, maderia land, was land that was granted to ex-or incumbent officials, war veterans, patriots or persons who were considered to have provided meritorious service to the crown in lieu of pension or salary. Such land was often granted for life, although the state held a reversionary right over it.

Holders of maderia land could operate the land themselves, or, as was most often the practice, lease it to tenants, or do whatever with it except pass it on to others by sale, gift, or mortgage. Most maderia land was heritable, but it was expected that the legatee remain loyal to the government and be ready to serve the crown. On the whole, the vast holdings of the state were primarily used for political purposes: by grants of land the reigning monarchs sought to buy support and loyalty, or by threats of dispossession, to discourage opposition.

Now, the tenure systems that we have discussed so far have one thing in common, namely that they all involve a reversionary right which was held not by the individuals operating the lands but by institutions—the corporate family or the village, the church, and the state. Rist, semon and maderia holders did not have final authority over the disposition of their lands, they only had usufruct rights. In each of these cases individuals could not sell their holdings,

---

[9]MLR: *Wollega* (Addis Ababa, 1968), p. 12
[10]MLR: *Kaffa* (Addis Ababa, 1969), p. 16

bequeth them as gifts or transfer them to others on mortgage. They could, however, pass them on to their heirs as inheritance, subject to the proviso noted in each case above, or lease them out to tenant cultivators.

From the standpoint of the recipients of rights of access to land, the difference among the tenures hitherto discussed is in the main one of form rather than content. It seems therefore more appropriate to divide the tenure system under the old regime into two broad categories, namely, *usufructuary tenures and private tenures*. The first could be further sub-divided into communal, church, and state tenures. The advantage of this scheme is two-fold: first, it simplifies what otherwise would be a highly involved and highly technical problem, and second, it does away with the conventional geographical classification, which divides the land system into that of the north and that of the south. Although private tenures were located predominantly in the south, usufructuare tenures, as we saw, were found in both regions of the country.

What we have so far called private tenures were originally lands which were expropriated from peasants and local chieftains in the south and given to officials and loyal servants of the crown. All unoccupied land in these areas was also considered to be state property which, through the years, was distributed to men of influence and power in the state apparatus. Much of the land thus acquired was subsequently converted into private tenure, and Haile Selassie's government accelerated this process by its policy of imperial land grants and by encouraging holders of state tenures to convert them into freehold. Land under private ownership could be sold or exchanged without any restrictions except those provided by law.

Lands under private tenures were private not in the strictly capitalist but in the specifically Ethiopian sense of the term. What the state had granted—and virtually all land under private tenures was originally state property—the state could take away, and in so far as the authority of the state was concerned, the sanctity of private property was not recognised in principle or in fact. In theory, all the land of the country belonged to the state, and under the ancient but obscure principle of 'eminent domain', the latter had the right to claim land held under private ownership, and to dispossess any person or landholding institution. In practice, however, this principle was rarely invoked.

Now, the concept of Ethiopian feudalism used by some writers appears inadequate in explaining the totality of the agrarian experience of the country before the land reform. This is because it not only blurs over the fact that the rural producers were made up of tenants as well as petty proprietors (as we shall see further down), but also that it underestimates the role of the state in agrarian relations.

In a country where land is the principal means of livelihood, and where the right of access to it is not ultimately held by the individual, the power of the authority—in our case the state—which decides how this resource is allocated will become overwhelming, and *all classes* of society will subordinate themselves to it. Under this condition, the state reaches into the private-economic life of everyone, and thus converts everyone, lord and peasant alike, into its *dependents*.

The state, in other words, becomes over-dominant and ceases to be the mere instrument of the landed classes.

In the case of the previous regime its over-dominance lay not only in its critical role in the allocation of resources, not only in its monopoly over the instruments of repression, but also because of a new element—the state apparatus. Haile Selassie's power was greatly inflated as a consequence of the modernisation and centralisation of the state apparatus. Modernisation left the land system and the role of the state in resource allocation largely unchanged.

Centralisation was superimposed on a traditional polity without disturbing existing social relations, or affecting the inherited prerogatives of the state. However, both processes removed the presence of the landed classes from the countryside, and transformed them from regionals war-lords into functionaries of the new bureaucracy, thereby cutting off their direct links with the peasantry. This explains in part the precipitate collapse of the aristocracy at the time of the land reform.

Tenancy and Petty Proprietorship

Let us return to our discussion of the land system. It is difficult to determine accurately how much of the country's cultivated area fell into usufructuary and private tenures in the sense that these two terms are defined above. It seems reasonable to argue that the area under usufructuary tenures was larger than that under private tenure. Both forms of tenure involved tenancy, although by far the largest percentage of tenant holdings was obtained from private owners.

The question of tenancy, its magnitude and characteristics needs to be considered carefully, the more so because the land reform put a great deal of emphasis on the assumption that the tenant was the most deprived and the most exploited member of rural society, which was true, and that tenancy was the most dominant form of land holding in the country, which is questionable. Once again, the paucity of accurate information makes it difficult to obtain a true picture of the extent of tenancy in the country. There is general agreement, however, that tenancy was much more widespread in the south than in the north. Gilkes has estimated that about 42% of all holdings in the country were tenant operated; this would mean that owner-operated holdings would be about 58%.[11] Cohen and Weintraub, on the other hand, state that 'well over half the peasants in the south' were tenants, and the southern peasantry, in their estimation, made up something like 60% of the country's rural producers.[12]

The last official agricultural survey to be carried out before the land reform swept away the old agrarian system was in 1974/75. The findings of this survey

---

[11]Gilkes, p. 115
[12]p. 51; this would mean that tenants were slightly over 30% of the country's rural population.

Table 2. *Distribution of Holdings by Tenure and Area Covered (%)*

Tenure	% of Total Holdings	% of Total Cropland Area
Communal	11	6
Owner-Operated	38	37
Tenant Operated	36	33
Owned and Rented	15	24

indicate that slightly over one-third of the holdings in the country, covering just about a third of the country's cropland area, were operated by tenant cultivators. The study uses a different classification from the one we have used here, but according to its findings the land holding pattern of the country on the eve of the land reform looked like this (figures have been rounded).[13]

It is obvious from Table 2 that a slightly higher percentage of holdings, covering a larger area of cropland was operated by owner cultivators. The figure will become much higher if we include those that operated partly owned and partly rented holdings.

The extent of tenancy varied from region to region as well as within regions and localities. It is important to bear in mind this inter- and intra-regional variation, for, as far as the beneficiaries are concerned, the outcome of the land reform has not been uniform everywhere as a consequence.

The data that is available, as well as our own findings, point to the fact that even in the south, tenancy was unevenly distributed, that in some areas there were a larger percentage of tenants, in others just the opposite. In Bolloso woreda, Wollaita awraja, for instance, we found that only about 20% of peasants were tenants before the land reform, and the rest, owner-cultivators. Although the evidence is lacking, there is good reason to believe that tenancy was quite low in the ensat culture complex extending from southern Shoa to northern Gamo Goffa. Moreover, significant variations were observed even within the same awraja. MLR's survey of Kaffa province, for example, shows that in Jimma awraja about 57% of all holdings were rented;[14] our own investigation of Manna woreda in the same awraja (which was not included in MLR's survey) reveals that about 36% of the peasants here were former tenants.

The landholding pattern shown in Table 3 is taken from the Ministry of Agriculture's study cited earlier. The study gives only regional figures, and we have selected the four regions where the woredas in which our field work was done are located.[15]

[13]Ministry of Agriculture: *Agricultural Sample Survey 1974/75*, vol. I, Addis Ababa, July 1975, p. 60. This and its accompanying vol. II shall hereafter be cited as *1974/75 Survey*; the second volume was published September 1975.

[14]MLR, *Kaffa*, op.cit.

[15]*1974/75 Survey*, vol. II, various pages.

Table 3. *Distribution of Holdings by Tenure in 4 Regions (%)*

Tenure	Regions			
	A	B	C	D
Communal	38	1	2	2
Private	42	34	28	69
Tenancy	2	48	57	27
Mixed	14	17	13	2

A=North-western Region (Gondar and Gojjam); B=Central-western Region (Shoa & Wollega); C=South-western Region (Kaffa & Illubabor); D=Southern Region (Sidamo, Bale, Gamo Goffa).

The table reveals that tenancy was very extensive in the central-western and south-western regions, while it was negligible in the north-western, and not quite as high in the southern regions. Owner-cultivators, on the other hand, were fairly widespread in all the four areas, being almost 70% in the southern region.

In dealing with the organisation of agricultural production, we must therefore not lose sight of the fact that both the small-holding owner-cultivator and the tenant were the backbone of the rural economy. Both lived in a world dominated by landlords and class privilege, and, in so far as the wider socio-political context was concerned, what they had in common far outweighed their differences. The field of power that surrounded them—to use Erik Wolf's apt expression—attentuated their narrow economic differences, and their relation to it was equally one of dependence and powerlessness. The same landlord, who as landlord collected rent from his tenants, was in turn local judge or administrator, and collected taxes and bribes from, and exercised control over, owner-cultivator and tenant alike.

While it is true that the small-holding owner was more secure in his holdings than the tenant, who was subject to eviction at any time, the difference was not an absolute one but one of degree. Powerful landlords, high government officials—and the two were often one and the same—and members of the royal household not infrequently dispossessed him just as easily as they turned their own tenants landless. But the one advantage that the owner-cultivator had over the tenant was that the former was free from the numerous contractual obligations the latter had to his landlord, although, all legally imposed taxes, including those for Health and Education, fell on both equally. As far as income and economic wellbeing was concerned, the difference between the two was not significant in qualitative terms. Both peasants were subsistence producers, they both employed the same traditional methods of cultivation, and the same primitive tools.

It must be pointed out, however, that the tenant carried a much heavier economic burden than his more fortunate counterpart. The general character of

24

Ethiopian tenancy and the conditions under which tenants laboured have been dealt with in a number of published works, and we shall therefore present here only a brief sketch.[16] The Ethiopian landless cultivator worked under a variety of constraints, chief among which were the following: 1. that he gave a major portion of his produce to the landlord in the form of rent; 2. that the form in which rent was paid acted as an obstacle to improvements in his production; 3. that he lacked security of tenure in his holding, and as a result, became powerless and incapable of making any kind of bargains to improve the terms of his contract, which were often verbal and not written.

There is general agreement that share-cropping was the most common form of rent payment throughout the country. What percentage of the peasant's produce was transferred as rent to the landlord, however, varied from area to area, as did the method of assessing the tenant's total output. In general, rent was between one-third to one-half of the harvest, depending on local custom, availability of land, and the fertility of the soil. What was standard throughout most of the country was that share rent was not a fixed and specifically determined quantity, but always a percentage or proportion of the harvest in a given season. Needless to say, the rent would be higher in a good year and lower in a bad one. This arrangement was on the whole unfavourable to the tenant, for while an exceptionally good harvest would enable him to retain a small surplus after paying his rent and taking care of his own needs, anything short of that would mean falling into debt, since what was left in his hands was insufficient to tide him over to the next harvest. Indebtedness was not uncommon among all peasants, and often the purpose of taking loans was basic–to buy food and clothing, to pay taxes and to purchase seeds for planting.

According to the available evidence, landlords played a minimal role in the production process. In many cases, they provided their tenants neither farm stock, implements nor seeds. The exceptions were among those landlords who resided close to the rural areas, who were either civil servants or business-men; these offered loans to needy peasants, usually at exorbitant rates of interest.

For all tenants, the major factor for their dependency, and the chief obstacle to improved production was the lack of security of tenure. Each share-cropper was never certain how long he would cultivate his holding, or when he would be told to give it up. To be sure, the practice of indiscriminate and recurrent evictions was not quite common, for this would have severely disrupted agricultural activity, and created dissatisfaction and unrest in the countryside. (We are not here referring to peasant evictions that occurred with the spread of mechanisation and commercial agriculture; we are referring to traditional, small-holding tenancy areas where mechanised farming had not yet appeared.) The threat of eviction, rather than the act itself, was the potent weapon in the hands of landlords, and the tenant over whom the danger of unemployment

[16]For a fuller treatment see references in footnote 1 on the first page of this section. My own short study summarises the findings of MLR; see 'Conditions of the Ethiopian Peasantry', *Challenge*, vol. X, No. 2, 1970.

and destitution hung like the sword of Democles had no alternative but to accommodate all the demands of his landlord, however onerous they were.

Tenancy agreements were often verbal, and based on the customary practices of each area; written or legally binding contracts were rare. The tenant could be relieved of his plot at any time except during harvest, and he was generally not compensated for any improvements he had made on the land. There were in fact cases where tenants were penalised for having made such improvements by being replaced by other tenants for a high rent.

The system of tenancy imposed severe limitations on developments in peasant agriculture, for the incentive for increased effort and better results were precluded by the internal logic of the system itself. The method of rent payment which penalised productiveness rather than rewarding it, the insatiable demands of landlords, and the consequent poverty of the tenant himself were factors which had a debilitating effect on production. In addition, the problem of security of tenure must be included as another severe constraint. The peasant who is secure in his holding will be more receptive to new ideas than the one who is bedevilled with uncertainty. Cohen and Weintraub strongly believe, however, that the prospects for tenants were not as dark as it seemed, that 'tenant farmers will adopt green revolution technology and improve their production when well planned agricultural projects are introduced.'[17] This might have been true in some instances.

In cases where local custom demanded that landlord-tenant relations be reasonably advantageous to both, where landlord and tenant belonged to the same community and the same culture, and where in addition the tenant was assisted by well planned extension programmes, the chances for better production were great. In most cases, however, the structural limitations of tenancy were too severe to be easily overcome.

The tenant did not often deal directly with his lord, but with the latter's local agent or sub-agent. The powerful landlords, who usually had hundreds of tenants in many parts of the country, did not reside in the rural areas, and absentee landlordism was an essential element of the agrarian system. The less powerful men of property, those that one might call the local gentry, lived in the proximity of their possessions and had frequent contact with their tenants.

The full extent of absentee ownership may never be known, and, we believe, the figures that are most often cited in this connection considerably underestimate the holdings of absentee owners. These figures, which are based on MLR's surveys for the provinces, are shown in Table 4.[18]

---

[17]p. 55
[18]MLR: *Draft Policy* ..., p. 10

Table 4. *Distribution of Absentee Ownership*

Province	Absentee Owners as % of Total Owners	Total Area Held by Absentee Owners (%)
Arssi	28	28
Bale	15	12
Gamo Goffa	10	42
Harar	23	48
Illubabor	42	42
Kaffa	18	34
Shoa	35	45
Sidamo	25	42
Wollega	29	28
Wollo	26	13

The Organization of Rural Production

Rural Ethiopia before the land reform was a land of smallholding peasants and of petty production. This might seem contradictory in view of the fact that a substantial portion of the rural wealth was held by big landlords and the state itself. But for reasons that we shall deal with in a moment, the normal practice was for landlords to rent out their property in small parcels to tenants and contract cultivators; large-scale, plantation-type enterprises were traditionally unknown and appeared only during the 1960s with mechanisation. This is an important point that has a bearing on the outcome of the land reform. The pattern of holdings that has emerged after land reform is by and large a close replica of the pattern of holdings of the old system.

To clarify the argument a brief comparison with the land system in Latin America may be helpful. In many Latin American countries, peasants are *denied access* to extensive land resources, which are instead controlled by big landlords and operated as haciendas or large-scale plantations. It has been estimated that more than 75% of the land in the continent belongs to about 10% of the population, and much of this land is given over to plantations. The majority of the peasantry is left to eke out a living on small plots, often of poor quality, by the side of the haciendas. In brief, by far the greatest portion of the resources of the rural world is *inaccessible* to the majority of the rural population. The argument of progressive Latin American intellectuals in favour of land reform is that an effective reform programme would convert land under the haciendas into peasant land, which would then enlarge the total *land fund* at the disposal of the peasantry, and consequently improve significantly the status and holdings of a great portion of rural society.

In contrast to their Latin American counterparts, the Ethiopian landed classes had for the most part parcelled up their property and leased them out to small holding cultivators. The peasantry had thus access to land, but this 'privilege' was acquired at a price which left the rural producer severely impoverished and powerless. The reason why the Latin American experience was not duplicated in Ethiopia had to do with the low level of development of rural production in the country, and the inability of the landed classes themselves to transform their holdings into large-scale plantations. The medieval form of cultivation, the archaic implements employed and the low level of agricultural know-how precluded anything but small-holding and petty production.

With the agricultural techniques and know-how available to him, the Ethiopian rural producer can effectively operate only a small plot of land. Some studies have suggested that the maximum that a peasant can efficiently farm is about 10 hectares.[19]

We believe that this is a bit too large for the average peasant and that 5 and 6 hectares of normal-quality land is about the size that such a peasant can handle fruitfully and efficiently. Since, for decades, indeed for centuries, the landed classes had no access to alternative agricultural technique and know-how superior to that of the average peasant, rural production had remained small-scale and decentralised. In a sense, and paradoxial as it may seem, the backwardness of the peasant had largely determined the organisation of rural production, and through this, the nature of the agrarian system.

To illustrate our point we shall cite figures obtained from official sources. The pre-land reform survey mentioned earlier breaks down, as we saw, the tenure system into four categories, and the average size of cultivated area per holding under these four in 1974 was: communal, 0.82 hectares; private, 1.49 hectares; tenancy, 1.38 hectares; and mixed holdings 2.33 hectares.[20]

General averages, however, do not provide a good enough picture of the problem at hand. Let us therefore look at the distribution of holdings by size for the whole country. The same document points out that about 58% of all holdings in the country were less than 1 hectare in size and accounted for about 18% of the total cropland area. Medium-sized holdings, i.e. those between 1 to 5 hectares, were 39% of the total and covered 52% of the cultivated area. Large holdings, those of 5 hectares and above made up 4% of total holdings and covered 29% of the area. The terms medium and large holdings as used here are taken from the same report.

It is interesting that the document itself classifies all holdings above 5 hectares as large holdings. A more appropriate classification would be to include holdings over 10 hectares only in this category. The publication does contain figures for land over this size, but unfortunately the maximum limit is not given. It is reasonable to suppose that under this class of holdings very few

---

[19]Henock Kifle: *Investigations on Mechanised Farming and Its Effects on Peasant Agriculture,* CADU Report No. 74, Assela CADU, 1972, p. 12. Also, Michael Ståhl: *Ethiopia: Political Contradictions in Agricultural Development.* Stockholm, 1974, p. 79.
[20]Ministry of Agriculture: *1974/75,* vol. 1; these figures, and the ones that follow appear on pp. 54–61.

Table 5. *Distribution of Holdings by Size and Area Covered (%)*

Holdings	Size in Hectares						
	Up to 0.10	0.11 −0.50	0.51 −1.00	1.01 −2.00	2.01 −5.00	5.01 −10.00	10.01 and above
Number	3.5	27.6	26.5	23.4	15.2	2.8	1.00
Area	0.2	5.8	12.4	22.3	30.0	12.1	17.2

Source: see Note 20.

plots would be over 20 hectares in size. Be that as it may, holdings over 10 hectares made up 1% of the total and accounted for 17% of the cropland area. A more detailed breakdown is shown in Table 5.

Another official report brings out the scattered and diminutive nature of peasant cultivation with great emphasis. According to the Central Statistical Office, which conducted its study between 1968 and 1971, not only was the country a land of small-holdings peasants but a large proportion of peasants, in many places the overwhelming majority, operated mini-plots of less than half a hectare in size. In Arssi, Bale and Gondar provinces, plots of less than half a hectare made up 49%, 59% and 60% respectively of total holdings. The largest percentage of tiny fields were found in Sidamo, Kaffa and Wollo, where 94%, 92% and 88% of holdings, respectively, measured less than half a hectare. In Harrar province, fields of this size covered 66% of the total.[21]

As we shall see later, the land reform affected all tenures equally. Not only were all peasants transformed into usufructuary holders, but all land in excess of 10 hectares in theory, but in practice of much smaller size, was taken away and distributed to the landless and the needy. In the distribution process, the lands of tenants as well as owner-cultivators were subject to alienation.

Although the old agrarian system was predominantly based on petty production and diminutive holdings, it was not all together immune from the corrosive influences of modern, large-scale farming. From the mid-1960s on, mechanised, or as it was often called, commercial agriculture, was making headway, and quite rapidly at times, in several parts of the country, including the coffee growing regions. There is a tendency on the part of some writers to exaggerate the magnitude of the 'capitalist offensive' in agriculture[22], and to view the emerging rationalisation of production as a kind of catastrophe. To begin with, commercial agriculture covered a small portion of the agricultural resources of rural Ethiopia—a rough estimate would be about 1 to 2% of the total cultivated

---

[21] CSO: *Results of the National Sample Survey, 2nd Round, vol. V, Land Area and Utilisation*, Addis Ababa, February 1975, p. 4.

[22] L. Bondestam made a mountain out of a mole hill, and in the process succeeded in demonstrating what every schoolboy knows, namely that change is often a painful experience, and that the new asserts itself at the expense of the old. See his 'Peoples and Capitalism in the North-eastern Lowlands of Ethiopia,' *Journal of Modern African Studies*, Vol. 12, No. 3, 1974.

area—and secondly, unless one took the position that the gods had forever doomed the country to stagnation and poverty, agricultural modernisation, with all its warts and blemishes, held some promise for improvements in the national economy. In any event, capitalist agriculture was at an infant stage when it was laid to rest following the upheavals of 1974 and the subsequent reforms of the military government.

The spread of mechanised farming posed a threat to peasants because it was often accompanied by severe disruptions in traditional agriculture and traditional ways of life. The first to feel the effects of mechanised agriculture were tenants, who were frequently evicted to make way for such operations, or were forced to pay higher rent on their holdings. A study in Arssi province, for instance, reveals that most of the peasants displaced by mechanised farming were tenants,[23] and the same was true in the Bako area between the borders of Shoa and Wollega provinces.[24] In general, commercial agriculture exacerbated the insecurity of all peasants, and in particular, aggravated the burden of tenant cultivators. Mechanised farms operated as islands in a sea of small-scale and traditional production, and there was rarely any positive interaction between one and the other. In addition, commercial agriculture brought no tangible and lasting benefit to peasant agriculture: all the know-how, the modern equipment and inputs, were inaccessible to the surrounding peasantry. The enterprises were strictly capitalist enterprises, and, although some seasonal employment was offered to peasants, particularly during harvest times, no serious attempt was made to provide assistance or advice to the neighbouring peasant population.

Other Limitations to Peasant Production

Although the problem of production in peasant agriculture was primarily structural, it also had to do with the extreme poverty—both material, and cultural in the Marxist usage of the term—of the peasants themselves. We have already shown, albeit briefly, the structural limitations of peasant production in the discussion above. It now remains to complete the picture by indicating the ancillary bottlenecks to improvements in peasant economy.

The limitations of the traditional Ethiopian means of cultivation—oxen and plough for cereal cultivation, hand tools for root crops—are all too well known to require extended treatment here. But what made the problem more serious was that a good portion of the peasantry did not own the essential tools of farm labour. This situation has not changed since land reform, and indeed in some areas it has worsened. The extent of scarcity of oxen and implements, but oxen in particular, varied from region to region, and from locality to locality within the same region.

---

[23]Henck Kifle, see pp. 20—22.
[24]Ståhl, *Ethiopia,* pp. 126—127.

According to the Ministry of Agriculture, in 1974 30% of all holdings in the country had no oxen at all, and only about 29% had a pair of oxen. It is not hard to imagine how seriously handicapped peasants without farm stock would be, especially if such peasants depend on cereal cultivation for their livelihood. Holdings with more than a pair of oxen, presumably of the better-off peasants, made up only 8% of the total.[25]

A great many peasants were thus not strong enough to stand on their own feet. They depended on others for farm animals and implements, and this assistance was offered usually in exchange for their labour or a portion of their harvest. Those without means of cultivation, which included both owner-cultivators and tenants, constituted the poorest section of the peasantry. These were the ones who were easily victimised by adverse natural conditions, and who often were forced to abandon their farms and migrate to urban areas in search of employment.

Another serious obstacle to improved production, one that has often been raised by many writers on the land question, was fragmentation. In the north as well as in the south, under all tenures, land fragmentation was widespread. The problem was in part tied to the prevailing system which often made it difficult for peasants to hold consolidated plots. In part, peasant attitude was also responsible for it because of the belief that it was advantageous to have several scattered plots.

In many farming communities, the unevenness of the quality of the land encouraged peasants to opt for fragmented holdings. A single peasant operating four to five, and in extreme cases as much as eight to ten, strips scattered in all directions, and each a good distance away from the other, was not uncommon. According to the findings of the Ministry of Agriculture, only 40% of holdings in the country were made up of single consolidated plots, whereas 36% consisted of 3 and more parcels.[26] The land reform has not dealt with this problem in any way, and in some localities in fact fragmentation has been further aggravated.

The reluctance of peasants to give up their traditional practices and to try new techniques must also be included as contributing to the poor record of rural production. In the 1960s, the government, with external assistance, launched extension and 'package' programmes to provide peasants with fertilisers, high-yield seeds, credit, and in some cases, to improve basic rural infrastructure. Undoubtedly, these programmes were far from adequate or properly administered; indeed, in some areas they brought hardship to the very people they were meant to benefit.[27]

Nevertheless, in a number of localities attempts were made to popularise

[25]Op.cit., vol. 1, p. 50.

[26]Ibid., p. 59.

[27]For a case study of three package programmes, see Michael Ståhl: *Contradictions in Agricultural Development. A Study of Three Minimum Package Projects in Southern Ethiopia*. Research Report No. 14. Uppsala: SIAS, 1973.

modern inputs and better methods of cultivation, but with very poor results. Today, only a small percentage of peasants use chemical fertilisers on a regular basis; improved methods of farming, better tools and labour-saving devices are practically unknown. As a result, agricultural output has been low, the average yield of peasant farms being about 6 to 8 quintals of cereals per hectare in the early seventies.

Although the backwardness and destitution of the peasantry was primarily not of its own making, but had its roots in the institutional framework of the prevailing system, the adverse consequences were always borne by the peasantry itself. Periodic and large-scale famine, malnutrition and disease often took a heavy toll of the rural population. In times of good rainfall and good harvest, the subsistence cultivator may be able to retain a small surplus after meeting all his obligations, but this was inadequate to enable him to make investments in his enterprise. In difficult times, he was quickly exposed to the hazards of starvation and disease.

There is general consensus that famine and starvation have stalked the Ethiopian people for a good portion of their history, but the fundamental reasons for this have not been fully explored. It is generally agreed that by the standards of many rural communities in Africa, Ethiopian peasants are considerably advanced in farm management and technique. Furthermore, that the Ethiopian rural producer is hard working, diligent, and competent within the limits of his knowledge has not been disputed by many. No less an authority on the agrarian question than Doreen Warriner had this to say about Ethiopian peasants: 'the ... peasant has developed very shrewd techniques of land and livestock management, and his native knowledge forms a very promising basis for development .... As compared with peasants in other developing countries, the highland peasants of Ethiopia are impressive in their industry and vitality ....'[28] And yet, the rural population has frequently been devastated, quite often in times of social stability, by acute food shortages and famine.

The worst famine in over half a century occurred in 1973, affecting several million people in the two provinces of Wollo and Tigrai. Men and women, young and old, peasants in their thousands perished in the disaster. Thousands dragged themselves to the nearby towns in search of food and assistance, quite a few of whom dying on the roadside, in the fields and city streets. While all this was taking place, often in full view of Ethiopians and foreign observers, government officials were frantically trying to convince their own people and the outside world that the tragedy was in fact a figment of the imagination of Ethiopia's ill-wishers, and that all was well in Wollo and Tigrai.

An accurate tally of the death and devastation caused by this catastrophe, which in the end was partly responsible for the downfall of the old regime, has not been made, and the exact number of victims may never be known. In 1975, the military government declared that about 200,000 peasants had perished,

---

[28]Cited in Cohen and Weintraub, Note 41, p. 25.

and this figure has not been disputed since then. Jack Shepherd estimated that by the end of 1973, the disaster had claimed more than 100,000 lives, and the 'politics of starvation' was the major reason why timely assistance was denied the people of the two provinces.[29]

The land reform has not solved the problem of famine which now has spread to other parts of the country, although efforts are being made to provide relief and rehabilitation. At present, that is by mid-1982, severely affected areas include parts of Harar province (the Ogaden), and areas in Bale, Sidamo, and Gamo Goffa. It seems therefore that the country will continue to be plagued with severe food shortages and malnutrition for a long time to come.

The great agricultural potential of the country so often cited by Ethiopians and foreign observers alike, has so far remained untapped. More realistic assessments have in fact painted a more sombre picture, warning that the country will come up against increasing difficulties in feeding its population. An unpublished FAO report, prepared in 1974, predicted that the country's agricultural prospects were bleak, that up to the mid-1980s food shortages, malnutrition and disease will continue to haunt the Ethiopian people, and these hardships will in return progressively aggravate the peasantry's destitution.[30]

Recent developments show that this dire warning cannot be taken lightly. It is now recognised that some areas of the country produce insufficient food to meet their own needs, and some others are barely self-sufficient. According to an unpublished report by the Agricultural Marketing Corporation (AMC), only four provinces, namely Arssi, Gojjam, Gondar and Shoa, produce surplus food grain, and that the rest of the other provinces are either grain deficit areas or produce only enough for local consumption.[31]

Social Classes in Rural Ethiopia

A few words on the class structure of rural Ethiopia on the eve of the fall of the old regime are now in order. A full and sustained discussion of classes and class conflict in this period is outside the scope of this work, although such endeavour is urgently needed in the light of developments since the overthrow of absolute monarchy and landlordism.

In dealing with the class formation of the Ethiopian countryside, however, we ought to be wary of schemes and formulas framed for social settings—such as China and Vietnam, for instance—whose content is different from that of

---

[29]*The Politics of Starvation*, New York, Carnegie Endowment, 1975, p. XII. This is mainly about the Wollo famine. For a report on the Tigrai famine, see Karl J. Lundström, *North-Eastern Ethiopia: A Society in Famine*, Research Report No. 34. Uppsala: SIAS, 1976.
[30]Cited in Shepherd, p. XII.
[31]AMC: 'Report on Grain Purchasing and Distribution' (in Amharic), Addis Ababa, unpublished mimeo, 1981.

Ethiopia. One writer has, for example, suggested that the social groupings that were important in the countryside were the following:[32]

Poor peasants: those operating the smallest holdings, i.e. up to 3 hectares.

Middle peasants: those operating from 3 hectares up to the maximum area which can be cultivated without using hired labour (10 hectares).

Rich peasants: those who themselves are cultivators but own additional land which they lease to tenants (10−20 hectares).

Landlords: people who own so much land that they do not have to practice agriculture themselves but can live on the rent from leased land (above 20 hectares).

The weakness of this analysis is in part that it confuses what is a *quantitative* difference for a *qualitative* one. The difference between one peasant who may have 3 hectares of land from another who may have 5 is a difference of degree, and not of *quality.* Just as the industrial worker who draws X units of money in wages is not in a different class from another who draws X+1, so the variations in size of holdings among peasant cultivators should not be the basis for classifying them into different social groupings. The essential factors that matter are the relation of the individuals to the means of production, and the nature of the productive process they are involved in.

All peasants who did not employ wage-labour but relied on their own efforts and those of their families, and who did not lease out their possession to others on a regular basis belonged to the same class, irrespective of how large or small their individual holdings might be. However, within this same class, one can distinguish two major substrata: those who had control over their means of production, namely, owner-cultivators, and those who obtained their means of production from others, namely tenants. In both groups, size of holdings varied from the smallest to the maximum which could be cultivated without hiring labour.

What would be more useful and closer to the reality of pre-reform Ethiopia is, we suggest, to divide rural society into four major social classes: the landed aristocracy, the local (landed) gentry, the peasantry, and the landless.

1. *The landed aristocracy.* Members of this class were powerful, often absentee, landlords who held positions of high authority in the state apparatus, who owned vast tracts of land and engaged a vast 'army' of tenants throughout the country. Although a few among them began to show interest in the more dynamic and more profitable mechanised agriculture towards the end of the 1960s, most were content to lease out their property to share-cropping cultivators, or to let them lie unused.

It is worth noting that during the crisis of 1974, what was believed to be the unassailable power of the aristocracy crumbled instead like a house of cards. To the surprise of everyone, this class put up virtually no resistance when it was

[32]Ståhl: *Ethiopia*, p. 88. A somewhat better analysis is provided by F.V. Goricke, *Social and Political Factors Influencing the Application of Land Reform Measures in Ethiopia,* Saarbrucken, Verlag, 1979, pp. 28−36, and 61−66.

stripped of its authority and its wealth. Moreover—and this too is a revealing point—whether in the urban areas or in the countryside, not a single hand was raised in its defence, not a single tear was shed in its downfall.

2. *The local gentry*. What distinguished this class from the previous one was not only that its possessions were much smaller, but that it led a different form of existence all together. Members of this class were often residents in the neighbourhood of their property and had more frequent contact with their tenants and the peasantry at large. A number of them were middle-level officials—judges, local administrators, etc.—while some were engaged in a variety of business activities.

Those landowners who were themselves cultivators, but had excess land which they leased out to tenants—owners of up to 20 hectares, on average—will have to be included in this class although their status was, in comparison, a lowly one.

In a great many cases, the local gentry in the southern provinces were 'outsiders', i.e. persons who were from the northern regions and culturally of Amhara-Tigrai stock. There were, however, gentry, or *balabats,* who were residents of and indigenous to the localities in which they held property.

The reaction of the local gentry to the policies of the military government was much different from that of the aristocracy. The strongest resistance to the land reform in 1975−1976 came principally from this class. In a number of rural areas, notably in Sidamo, northern Shoa and Wollo, local landlords launched armed opposition in an attempt to frustrate the implementation of the reform, and on a few occasions they were successful enough in raising a considerable following. Although their opposition was not strong enough to actually threaten the military regime, it was serious enough to alarm it, and the resistance continued for a while before it was finally crushed.

3. *The peasantry*. Both small-scale free holders and tenants are included in this class which formed the overwhelming majority of the rural population. We have already dealt with the peasantry in the discussion above, and there is no need to go back over the same points.

4. *The landless*. The most deprived sector of the rural population were the landless, who had no land to cultivate, who had no oxen, farm implements or livestock of any kind, and who led a marginal existence. Quite often, they were absolutely destitute, and they managed to survive only by occasional employment on commercial farms, construction projects or, as was frequently the case, by helping out on farms of relatives or neighbours in exchange for food and other assistance. One estimate has put the total number of landless households in the rural areas at slightly over 400,000[33].

It will be observed that we have left out agricultural wage-labourers and commercial/capitalist farmers from our scheme of analysis. This is deliberate, for neither of these two groups was numerically or socially significant enough to be identified as a class. In the case of the former, many were landless peasants,

---

[33]Gilkes, p. 115.

or holders of mini-plots whose land was too small to meet their needs, and who took up employment to supplement their income.

The relative strength of each of these classes is impossible to determine with any degree of accuracy. The two landed classes—the aristocracy and the local gentry—were undoubtedly numerically insignificant, but together they weilded enormous political and economic power in rural society. However, although a good portion of the local gentry had greater contact with the peasantry, neither of the two classes could be said to have had a strong or permanent presence within the peasant community, and their control over their property was often indirect, that is through agents and superintendents. What the land reform did was to eliminate the landed classes as a whole politically, and at the same time to remove from them their juridical right over the land. Furthermore, what made the implementation of the reform relatively easy was that all or almost all of the land of the propertied classes was already in the hands of the peasantry.

Chapter 3

The Land Reform

3.1 The Legislation

The Reform Proclamations, 1975–82

Proclamation No. 31 of 1975, which is entitled 'Public Ownership of Rural Lands Proclamation' is the first and central legislation which set off the process of land distribution and the organisation of peasants in Peasant Associations. There has been other legislation since then regarding rural lands, the most recent being in May 1982, but none have made any major alterations in the first proclamation. This latter thus remains the basic document of the country's agrarian reform.

The document expresses the hope that the reform will serve the goals of economic development in general, and rural development in particular. The basis of this development is founded upon a new agrarian order in which the independent small-holder will become the major force in rural production, and in which in-equalities of wealth and possession will be eliminated as far as possible.

It is not quite clear what exactly is meant by 'public ownership of rural lands', although the exclusion of private property is implicit in the term, and has been spelt out in the proclamation. The nearest attempt at a definition is in Article 3 which states in general terms that 'all rural lands shall be the collective property of the Ethiopian people'. One possible interpretation could be that the state, as the *de facto* surrogate of the people, and the ultimate political authority, will have final jurisdiction over the disposition of rural land. The authority of the Peasant Associations to administer the land in their areas is, in the final analysis, an authority delegated to them by the central government.[1]

Article 4 contains the most important provisions of the proclamation. Private ownership of land by individuals or organisations, are prohibited; so, too, the transfer of land by sale, lease, mortgage or similar means.

Thus the law acknowledges only the use right, or usufructuary possession, of the cultivator over his holding. Any person who is 'willing to personally

---

[1]The other proclamations pertaining to the land reform, all published in the official *Negarit Gazeta*, are the following: Proclamation No. 71, Dec. 1975 (on Peasant Associations); No. 77 of 1976, as amended by No. 152 of 1978 (on agricultural income tax); No. 130, Sept. 1977 (on formation of nation-wide Peasant Associations); and No. 223, May 1982 (on restructuring Peasant Associations).

cultivate land shall be allotted rural land sufficient for his maintenance and that of his family.' The maximum size of land for each self-labouring rural household shall 'at no time exceed 10 hectares'.

The emphasis on owner-cultivation is brought out in sub-article 5 where the use of hired labour to cultivate one's holding is prohibited.

Another important provision of the new law appears in Article 6. This finally abolishes the onerous practice of tenancy, and frees the peasant from all obligations to the landlord.

Land in excess of 10 hectares, and large-scale mechanised farms were to be expropriated without compensation, except for 'movable properties and permanent works on the land'. Despite the caveat, no compensation was ever paid to landlords for any property they lost. Mechanised farms were to be organised into state farms or cooperatives, or parcelled up and distributed to peasants.

With regard to rist areas, one special provision was included, namely that no non-resident was henceforth entitled to put in claims to land (Article 20). As far as nomadic areas were concerned, the people in the area were given 'possessory rights over the lands they customarily use for grazing and other purposes related to agriculture', and any obligations they may have had to balabats and traditional chiefs were cancelled.

Article 28 annuls all cases involving land disputes before the ordinary courts. It further specifies that cases involving rural lands shall henceforth not be brought before the regular courts. This thus deprived the corruption-ridden judicial authorities in the countryside their power and much of their unlawful sources of private gain.[2]

The proclamation also set up Peasant Associations (PAs). Each PA was to be organised on an 800-hectare area, and membership was to be made up of tenants, landless labourers, owners with less than 10 hectares, and, after the completion of land distribution, former landlords who were willing to personally cultivate their holdings. PAs were given a wide range of functions and responsibilities, chief among which were the following: to administer public property; to establish service co-operatives; to build schools and clinics; and to undertake villagisation programmes. Initially, however, their major function was to implement the land reform.

PAs were also empowered to establish *judicial tribunals*. These were initially concerned with cases involving land disputes among PA members, but later their powers were widened considerably.

Proclamation No. 31 also made provisions for Peasant Associations to be organised at the woreda and awraja levels, the former to be made up of delegates from PAs within the woreda, and the latter, delegates from each woreda in the awraja. Judicial tribunals were also similarly organized.

Subsequent legislation has considerably broadened the scope of PA powers

---

[2]For a more detailed discussion of the Proclamation, see Befekadu Degefe: *Economic Effects of Nationalisation—Distribution Policy,* Unpublished manuscript, Faculty of Law, Addis Ababa University, June 1978, part II.

and duties. Proclamation No. 71 of December 1975 empowered associations to establish producers cooperatives, defence squads, and also women's associations. It was pointed out here that the aim of government policy was 'to enable the peasantry to administer itself'. The defence squad, the leadership of which was to be elected by the general assembly of the PA, was to be the law enforcing agent of the peasant community. It was its responsibility to execute the decisions of judicial tribunals and to carry on 'necessary security and defence activities'. Additional powers were also given to judicial tribunals. They were empowered to hear civil as well as criminal cases, and to impose penalties of up to 300 Birr or 3 months in jail.

The PA is a mass organisation composed of all peasants in the community over 18 years of age. Its *general assembly* is the highest decision-making authority, and elects the leadership of all subsidiary bodies as well as its own executive council. More importantly, PAs have assumed many of the functions of the old local administrative apparatus of the previous regime. It is the PA which is responsible for collecting taxes, resolving community conflicts, providing services and maintaining law and order. The agrarian reform has thus drastically restructured rural society, and promises the peasant the opportunity to administer his own affairs.

In 1977, the government decided that PAs must be etablished at the provincial and national levels, the provincial PAs to coordinate the activities of all lower level PAs in the provinces, and the national organisation––the All-Ethiopian Peasant Association (AEPA)–to be responsible for the work of all the country's PAs.[3] Members to AEPA are elected by the general assemblies of their respective provincial PAs, and members to the latter by assemblies of their awraja organisations, and so on down to the woreda and local or *kebbelle* level. The kebbelle Peasant Association is the basic organisational unit of the rural community, the grass roots organisation which is charged with administering the land in its area, and responsible for the basic needs of the peasant community.

In summary, the reform legislation is radical in content, and involves important changes in the system of land holdings and in the social profile of rural Ethiopia. It has abolished landlordism, tenancy, the hiring of labour, and envisages a self-labouring peasantry of small-holders, all of whom have only possessory or usufructuary right over the land they cultivate. All land resources and rural assets are 'the collective property of the Ethiopian people'. In the rist areas, the abolition of recurrent land claims and therefore of the 'corporate' family system, discussed above, is bound to have profound social and familial implications. In the South, and especially the tenancy areas, the elimination of landlordism, and the removal of 'outsiders' who previously exercised control over the land of the indigenous population, will do away with some of the causes of ethnic discontent which was common in the past.

---

[3] PMAC: *Negarit Gazeta,* Proc. No. 130, 17 September 1977.

3.2 The Process of Land Distribution

Introduction

> In its narrower and most popular sense, 'land reform' means the redistribution of land. This is the type of reform which arouses the deepest political passions, for in a predominantly agrarian society a redistribution of land means a redistribution of wealth, of income, of status and political power, in short, a revolutionary change in the social structure.
>
> U.N.: *Progress in Land Reform, Fourth Report.*

This view is shared by a good many students of agrarian reform, and the subject—both in theory and practice—has indeed aroused deep political passions. Radical proponents of reform have often prescribed thorough-going measures, arguing that only such measures will make it possible to carry through the transfer of wealth and power from the propertied classes to the producing ones. It is presumed that these latter, that is, the direct producers, will use their newly acquired privileges for the benefit of society at large. 'Agrarian reform is like deep surgery'—this catch phrase has been echoed in a variety of ways in the radical literature on the agrarian question.[1]

A number of historical experiences have, however, shown that the practical outcome of reforms has not always confirmed what has been claimed in theory. Practice, in fact, reveals complex problems and issues that have not often been anticipated in theory. The value of case studies, such as the kind we are attempting here, is therefore to uncover what is particular and unique in each specific experience, and to point out the limitations of generalised models.

In this and in the sections that follow, we shall discuss the process and outcome of land distribution (the 'distribution of wealth'), and the evolution and status of rural organisations (the 'redistribution of power'). But before that a few words about the problems of land distribution.

Both before and after the October Revolution, Lenin strongly argued that in essence land reform is not a socialist programme, but rather a bourgeois-democratic one. He insisted that the proletarian revolution must accept the hard fact that rural production, particularly where the peasantry was politically and culturally backward, will take quite a while to be socialised. Unlike industrial production, which the victorious proletariat can immediately restructure along socialist lines, peasant production will remain petty-bourgeois

---

[1] The phrase is by Flores; in addition, see Lehmann and the essays in Stavenhagen. For a different viewpoint, see Dorner, Tai, Tuma and Warriner. A brief exposition of the Marxist debate appears in de Janvry, especially ch. 3. For the Soviet experience, see Hussain and Tribe. *The Journal of Peasant Studies* carries interesting debates on the agrarian question from a variety of perspects, and also case studies of many experiences. Agrarian reform has also been seen as the foundation of political democracy. See Ladejinsky's papers in Walinsky (ed.).

and petty for a considerable period of time. With the introduction of NEP in 1921, Lenin's views became party policy, and the Bolshevik state accepted as a transitional measure the coexistence of a dual economy, a nationalised industrial sector side by side with a private rural sector.

Lenin's arguments and their implications for policy have not been seriously considered in the contemporary Marxist debate on the agrarian question. As a consequence, not enough attention has been given in the literature to the process and problems of land distribution.

To the extent that agrarian reform remains a pre-socialist programme (or a *long-term* pre-condition for socialism), to the extent it aims to free rural society from *archaic* productive relations, the rational redistribution of rural assets becomes one of its central concerns. Redistribution involves the improvement of the status and conditions of the majority of rural society, in particular its least privileged sector. The major beneficiaries or reform will need to be landless peasants, peasants with insufficient means and, where tenancy or share-cropping exists, those involved in contractual arrangements.

On the other hand, redistribution must ensure that the interest of the small, independent owner-cultivator is at least preserved, or preferably, ameliorated. But this is easier said than done, particularly so in areas where land is a scarce resource—which is the case in most countries, Ethiopia included—and the population pressure is very high. A hasty and unplanned distribution may actually hurt those that the reform was meant to benefit, and may create a class of dissatisfied or embittered peasants. The process of land distribution is therefore a complicated and delicate operation, and must be carried out with great care and, above all, with the full participation of the rural community itself. However, even if land reform is carried out under the most favourable conditions, and with the active support of all concerned, there is still no guarantee that the programme will be fully successful, and that there will be universal satisfaction among the beneficiaries.

Land Distribution: Measures

Land redistribution was an important aspect of Ethiopia's land reform, but initially it was carried out under unfavourable and uncertain political conditions, and without expert advice or the active involvement of the rural population. The general social climate in the countryside in 1975 was unsettled, and the direct and indirect opposition of the landed classes to the reform had created civil discord in a large number of rural communities. The peasantry itself was uncertain about the content and implications of the reform and, characteristically and justifiably, had adopted a cautious attitude.

The first act of implementation of the reform was the organisation of Peasant Associations and, in a haphazard and hasty manner, the distribution of land within each Peasant Association area. This task was in the main carried out under the guidance of *zematcha* participants who, for the most part, were ignorant of rural life and the complexities of local conditions. Since then, that is, since the first attempt in 1975 and 1976, Peasant Associations (PAs) themselves have designed and pushed through fresh redistribution of land, partly to correct imbalances, and partly to accommodate new members of PAs who have become eligible to a share of land in the years since the organisations were formed.

In many areas, PAs have been pressured to engage in periodic redistribution of land, or carry out major measures of readjustment, by the land reform itself. Although the legislation does not directly encourage it, certain of its provisions have made recurrent redistribution or readjustment unavoidable. The main reasons for this are the following:

1. The area within the jurisdiction of each PA has been legally determined––a maximum of 20 *Gashas* (or 800 hectares)—and cannot be changed without the express permission of a host of higher authorities. Changing PA boundaries is, in any event, a complicated and difficult task—in a way similar to changing national boundaries—and most PAs and higher authorities are unwilling to be involved in it. However, not all the land within a PA area is cultivatable since some of it may consist of woodland, marshy areas, rocks, hills, and the like.

All this means is that the arable land available to each PA is fixed and limited, but the membership of the association expands from year to year, and at a rate determined by a host of demographic factors. A resident of a PA community becomes eligible to membership of the PA, and therefore to a share of land, at the age of 18. Since new, unused land is either scarce or unavailable, new members will acquire land only if land redistribution is carried out and some of those with larger plots are made to give up portions of them to others. Since the reform of 1975, the membership of PAs has grown by 9% in Bolloso, 18% in Manna, 14% in Adet and 19% in Sire.

2. Since land cannot be transferred by sale, lease, inheritance (except to minors and widows), or other means, there is no other way of acquiring it except through the PA. In addition, to bring virgin land into cultivation requires capital and effort beyond the ability of the average peasant or PA.

3. Peasants are reluctant or unwilling to move out of their own communities, and therefore 'colonisation' of unclaimed land is not very popular. Moreover, unclaimed land is often land that a peasant with the know-how and technique available to him cannot profitably operate. The peasant who is about to set out on his own is very often absolutely destitute. He does not own the implements, oxen, seeds, and other basic items necessary for farming. He therefore depends on relatives and friends for the first two or three harvests. In an alien environment, far from his sources of assistance and support, he will be exposed to the threats of starvation.

The problem of recurrent redistribution or readjustment is one which all PAs face in one way or another, more or less acutely, depending on their natural endowments. On the one hand, PAs attempt to provide everyone with a means of livelihood, on the other they are saddled with a fixed and unchanging *land fund* and an ever-growing population. Some of the localities we studied had had as many as four redistributions since 1975, some others as few as two.

Let us look at the problem of redistribution more closely in our four woredas, but first a few general comments. The method of land distribution, and the criteria used varied not only from one locality to another but within each locality as well. Indeed, each PA adopted its own formula and decided how and to whom to apportion land within its jurisdiction. The decisions in each case were not arbitrary, on the contrary, the took into account the quantity and quality of land available for distribution, the degree of landlessness and land-hunger in the community, and the general attitude of the people. It may be said that peasants and peasant leaders involved in land apportionment made attempts not to violate the traditional norms of justice and fairness accepted in the rural community. The general feeling was—and this was brought out to us in our discussions with peasants who had been active—that as far as possible everyone should be accommodated, that the landless and the land-hungry should be given a share, and that if there was not enough land for everyone, then some of the fortunate ones who had larger plots should give up portions of them for the benefit of their less fortunate neighbours. Traditional justice is however far from perfect or blameless, although it is accepted by the peasant community. A certain degree of partiality to oneself, to relatives or close friends, and even a certain degree of venality is tolerated in practice so long as it is not blatant or taken to extremes.

It must be pointed out that after the first attempt at land apportionment carried through under the influence of Zematcha participants, the task was accomplished in the main by peasants and PAs themselves. This was by default rather than by design. Since the government did not have trained rural agents to send to the tens of thousands of PAs involved in the distribution process, it was left to the peasants themselves to carry out the task. This has contributed greatly to the success of land distribution.

The most common practice was that before distribution took place a general assembly of the PA, that is, a gathering of all members in the community, was called. The general assembly meetings, which are usually infrequent and poorly attended, attract at such times all members, and arguments and debates are sharp, and often acrimonious. Most peasants, though sympathetic to the plight of their less fortunate colleagues, do not wish to lose what they already have. The assembly decides on a number of crucial issues: 1. whether to create a special distribution committee for that purpose, or authorise the governing body of the PA to carry out the task; 2. whether to invite government officials at the local office as observers or not; 3. who should be given priority, and what methods should be used for land allocation.

The distribution process is a complicated one, and can never be perfect. Not all peasants were satisfied with the eventual outcome of the distribution. Some felt they were entitled to larger plots, others that they had not been treated fairly. Some complained that those involved in allocation of plots were guilty of favouritism, nepotism and the like, others that the whole endeavour had been to the benefit of one social group and not to all ... etc. One particular source of friction had to do with the fact that peasant leaders, or those in charge of land allocation, had no accurate means of land measurement, so that there was a great deal of disagreement on the actual size of a given plot. Visual estimates, which often served as means of measurement by the distributors were often contested by others. Nevertheless, despite the complaints and dissatisfactions, serious conflicts or social tension did not occur, at least not in the areas of our study.

The distribution process did not aim to bring about the complete equalisation of the holdings of everyone, for this was impossible due to factors such as family size, previous status and size of holdings, the quality of the land, the farming ability of the individual, (i.e. whether he was a capable farmer and had the means requisite for cultivation), and so on. As far as the distributing agents were concerned, the main purpose was to accommodate everyone as much as possible, and to eliminate what all peasants consider to be the greatest misfortune, namely landlessness.

Below we present some of the measures adopted for land distribution in the areas in our study.

Bolloso. The cultivable area under the jurisdication of PAs, that is, the total *land fund,* is on the whole extremely small. What is more, the reform did not enlarge the land fund of the woreda so that land allocation was more a form of adjustment of holdings and accommodation of the landless and the land-hungry rather than a total and complete redistribution. The largest cultivable area, controlled by one PA, was 21 Gashas, and the smallest, 8 Gashas. Of the nine PAs we studied, four of them possessed between 8 and 10 Gashas of arable land, and another four about 12 Gashas each. The last land distribution in the area took place in 1976, 1977 and 1978. In most cases, the leadership of the PAs, and not a specially designated distribution committee, was responsible for reapportionment. What were the criteria used for allotting land to individuals? The following were among the most common measures adopted by the PAs.

1. Land was distributed on the basis of family size and those with larger households were given larger plots. This was a straightforward measure which excluded considerations such as quality of land, previous status, etc.

2. Priority was given to the landless and the land-hungry. Here family size was not taken into consideration, since the concern was to allot plots to those who were destitute. The land-hungry are those with insufficient land.

3. Where land was extremely scarce, and claimants rather numerous, apportionment took place on the following basis:

(a) landless peasants were given plots without taking family size into account;

(b) the plots of land-hungry peasants were increased on the basis of the size of their households;

(c) former tenants were allowed to cultivate the plots they already possessed.

The excess land that became available for distribution was acquired from holders who were thought to have larger plots.

4. Some land was taken from those who were considered to have large holdings, and distributed to those who were thought to be land-hungry. The amount of land lost by large holders was based on family size, that is, those with larger households lost less than those with smaller households.

The term 'large-owner' must be taken in its relative sense. In Bolloso, and Wollaita in general, where average holdings are tiny, a peasant who works 1 to 1.5 hectares is considered a large owner.

As the membership of each PA expanded with the infusion of new members, the demand for land, and hence re-apportionment, became greater, and it was quite evident that PAs were in no position to accommodate everyone. Through our discussions with local officials and development agents we learnt that some PA leaders had approached the local administration to suggest that a settlement or 'colonisation' scheme be devised by the government to settle the newer members of their PAs and to relieve the growing pressure on their limited resources. Peasant leaders on the whole consider that with the acute shortage of land, any measure of land allotment would mean that a greater percentage of peasants would be losers, and only a small percentage beneficiaries.

This problem had emerged in its most acute form not only in Bolloso but also in Manna.*

Manna. The size of arable land under the control of PAs here too is quite small, although on the average, Manna is slightly better off than Bolloso. The gap between the smallest and the largest PA is fairly wide, the former being 8 Gashas, and the latter 27. Of the total of 10 PAs under our study, 6 held land ranging in size between 8 and 15 Gashas, far below the legally set limit of 20 Gashas. For distribution purposes, the land was divided into two categories: coffee land and grain land, the latter for cereals and vegetables. Each member of a PA was entitled to a share from both categories of land.

The actual land allocation was carried through by a distribution committee elected by each PA. However, each committee included members of the governing body of the PA, and as a result, was considered by many peasants not as an independent body but as one subordinate to the PA leadership. Here, as in Bolloso, redistribution has given rise to a continual process of diminution of plots. Redistribution has been going on for some time, the latest one as recently as 1981.

---

*The chairman of Manna Woreda PA informed us that henceforth the only way plots could be available for distribution to new PA members was if a member who already held land died or left the community for good in which case his land would revert back to the PA which can then allocate it to landless members.

In addition to family size and accommodation of the landless—measures similar to Bolloso—distributors in Manna used the following criteria:

1. A ceiling was fixed for the minimum and maximum size of plots to be allotted to members of PAs. The ceiling varied from one PA to another. The minimum was given to a single-member household, and a given unit of land (this also varied among PAs) was added for each additional member up to the maximum ceiling set by the PA.

2. A ceiling was fixed for the maximum size of household to be considered for land allocation. Any addition to a household above the set ceiling (often between 6 and 8) was disregarded.

The ceiling on the number of children was adopted for understandable reasons. Not only was the land available for distribution limited, but the population in the area is predominantly Moslem, multiple marriages are quite common, and as a result the average size of households tends to be quite large. Indeed, some PAs who had attempted to use family size as the basis of land allotment found that it was quite difficult to determine what a family or a household was. Some strongly argued that a household consisted of all the 'dependents' of a household head. This meant that a peasant who had several wives in different places had a distinct advantage over another who had only one, and land allotment on this bases would create a privileged sector of 'polygamous large-owners'.

The issue became quite contentious because it was tied up with religion and custom. On the other hand, there was apprehension that those who argued in favour of the 'polygamous' position—and they were a significant minority––were far more interested in acquiring more land, particularly coffee plots, than in the welfare of their multiple households. The long-term implications of accepting it as the basis of land allocation was also viewed as unhealthy. It was finally decided to define a household as 'those who live and eat together'. But this did not completely solve the problem, for some peasants brought all their children by their different wives under one roof, leaving the wives to fend for themselves as best they could. It was this that forced some PAs to put a ceiling on the number of children to be considered for land allocation. One PA which carried out its latest redistribution in 1980 decided that henceforth children born to families will be disregarded in future land allocations.

Adet. Conditions in Adet and Sire were somewhat different, and in some ways better than the two woredas discussed above. In Adet, the shortage of land was not as acute as in the previous places. The smallest PA in terms of land size had 600 hectares (about 15 Gashas) of arable land as compared with the other areas where the comparable size was 8 Gashas. Indeed, most of the PAs in Adet controlled well over the legally prescribed maximum, the largest of them having close to twice this size. However, the quality of land varied considerably from locality to locality, and quite a good portion of the woreda was inaccessible and inhospitable.

Adet was slow to implement the land reform, and it was only in 1980 and

1981 that some form of land distribution was carried out. This is true of the *rist* areas, in some of which actual large scale land distribution had not taken place by 1981. But in Adet, reapportionment was accompanied by PA restructuring and the redrawing of PA boundaries. Some of the PAs in our study were going through this restructuring process at the time of our study and some of them had just completed it when we started.

The reapportionment process here was more organised and orderly than in the other areas of our study. In addition, because the rist system, which was in practice in Adet before the reform, tended to minimise landlessness, and to some extent tenancy, the distribution here was largely a form of readjustment of holdings and accommodation of land-hungry peasants. The result was that there was less levelling here than in the two other areas, although a certain degree of dispossession of larger holders and upgrading of smaller holders did take place.

All PAs in the area selected distribution committees which were given full authority to make final decisions on allocation of plots. The leadership of the PAs were excluded from membership in the committees, but were allowed to be observers. Peasants who felt unfairly treated had the right to appeal their case, but very few peasants took the offer because the process of litigation was complicated, time consuming, and the chances of success very limited. Although the distribution process appears to be more democratic in comparison with the other areas in our study, mainly because it was carried out by an independent body elected by the peasants themselves, complaints of malpractice against the distributors were far more common here than in the three other woredas.

The measures for allotment adopted in Adet were somewhat less complicated than those in the previous areas, namely:

1. Allotment was made on the basis of family size and the quality of land. Each household receiving land had a share from both the good as well as the poor land available for distribution.

2. A minimum ceiling of a unit of land (the minimum varied among PAs) was set for a household, and any addition over this was based on the number of household members. Here too, all shared from the good and the poor land in the PA *land fund*. Each additional member of a household had at least two parcels—good and poor quality—to add to the family. The need to provide everyone with the proper balance of good and poor quality land resulted in a number of cases in the dispossession of larger holders of portions of their land.

Sire. The experience of Sire falls in between those areas with high population density and land shortage such as Bolloso and Manna, and those areas where such problems are relatively less acute such as Adet in the north. The lands controlled by PAs here are neither large nor unduly small, the largest size of arable land under a PA being 28 Gashas, the smallest 10, with most PAs possessing land between 15 and 20 Gashas. Sire PAs were not too eager to initiate land redistribution, and as a result, the frequency and extent of land distribution was fairly limited. Out of 9 PAs we investigated, 5 had not had redistribution except for some readjustment and accommodation of landless peasants since the proclamation of 1975. The four other PAs which had actually carried out redistribution had done so only once.

The distribution when it took place was carried out by the leadership of the PAs themselves. Among the measures adopted for land allotment the following are unique to Sire:

1. Land was apportioned to the landless and the needy, but in doing so care was taken to assign plots which were closer to claimants' homesteads. This was partly to avoid land fragmentation and partly to enable peasants to work as close to their homes as possible. In this instance, the quality of the land was not taken into account.

2. Land was apportioned on the basis of ability to farm. Households with the requisite oxen, tools and 'farm hands' were given enough land for their maintenance; those without these basic items of cultivation were given smaller plots.

Most of the PAs here encouraged former tenants and owner cultivators to carry on working the land in their possession and to consolidate their plots. The methods adopted in Sire have had at least one advantage, namely, fragmentation of peasant holdings has been reduced considerably. In contrast, the process of distribution in the other areas has aggravated this problem, and made fragmentation a permanent feature of the new agrarian structure.

The process of distribution in the four areas in our study—as in all areas in the country—varies greatly in substance as well as in detail in accordance with local conditions and previous experiences. However, there are also commonalities shared by all. To begin with, distribution took place with the resources already available. The land reform *did not enlarge the land fund* at the disposal of PAs in any appreciable way, except to a small degree in Manna (with the appropriation of small coffee plantations). Secondly, in all cases, the landless and the land-hungry were given some land which in the nature of things was taken from larger peasants. *The result of the distribution, which we shall discuss at length in the next section, was a levelling down, more or less extensive, depending on the pattern of holdings prior to the reform in each locality, and the total land fund at the disposal of each PA.*

Insofar as owner-cultivators and former tenants were concerned, distribution in all areas has meant one of the following:

1. Where the shortage of land was not severe, peasants in both categories were allowed to hold on to their previous plots; in a few cases, the poorer among them were allotted additional land.

2. Where there was not enough land to accomodate everyone, owner-cultivators and former tenants, especially the former, were made to give up some of their land for distribution to others.

One point which should be emphasised is the purpose of land distribution as understood by the peasants themselves. To peasants in many parts of the country, and certainly to those in our woredas, land is a scarce resource, and the life-line of the rural producer. The general intent of peasant leaders and peasants involved in land distribution was to allot plots to all, which as far as possible would cover the most basic needs of the cultivators and their families. This is in line with Article 4—1 of the first proclamation, although the end result would have been the same had there been no such provision in the law.

As was noted above, the distribution process was accomplished primarily by the peasants themselves. While the result is by no means perfect, and while grumbling and dissatisfaction in some sectors of the peasantry about unfair treatment in the hands of those charged with land allotment are often to be heard, the kind of acute conflict and civil discord associated with a task of this nature has by and large not taken place. The completion of the distributive process—on the whole successfully—is a considerable achievement of peasant cooperation.

Land Distribution: Eligibility.

Who was eligible for land allotment and who was not? Every head of a household, permanently resident within the jurisdictional area of a PA, is entitled to be a member of the organisation and must register as such. Although membership is not compulsory, peasants choose to register because the advantages far outweigh the disadvantages. The basic unit of the rural community as well as that recognised by the PAs is the family or household. A peasant is registered as a number of a PA not just on his own behalf but on that of his household. This does not mean that young peasants, who may be single, are excluded. As soon as such peasants come of age (i.e. reach 18 years) and establish their own homestead, they become accepted as heads of a household and thus members of the PA. That they are not married is of no consequence, since everyone expects that this 'deficiency' will soon be removed. Indeed this is not a problem at all, because peasants are often married by the time they become eligible for membership.

Under existing socio-cultural practices, it is the *male* member of the household who is accepted as *household-head;* it is he who is registered on behalf of the family in the PA, and in whose name land allotment is made. In effect, therefore, rural women are excluded from PA membership and, consequently, cannot acquire land in their own right. The exceptions are widows, divorcees, and those whose husbands have, for one reason or another, temporarily left the community. We found, for instance, that only 6% of the household-heads listed in PA registers in Bolloso, and 10% of those similarly registered in Adet were women, a great majority of whom elderly widows. The figures for the other two areas are much smaller.

Article 4 (para. 1) of the first proclamation reads as follows: 'without differentiation of the sexes, any person who is willing to personally cultivate land shall be allotted rural land sufficient for his maintenance and that of his family'. The intent of this passage appears to be that land should be allotted to any person irrespective of sex, that men as well as women are entitled to a share of land in their community. If the land reform had been actually implemented along these lines, the difficulties during land distribution would have been far greater than they actually were. In addition, abuses would have been harder to control, particularly in areas where multiple marriages were prevalent. In these areas, men-peasants would register their wives in more than one PA and acquire land for *themselves*, since social customs oblige women in many rural cultures to surrender property to their husbands. Furthermore, women in almost all areas of the country are customarily prohibited from engaging in some forms of farm work, such as ploughing and sometimes sowing, although their participation in all other forms of farm labour more than matches that of their husbands. This would have meant that in the end the control of the land would have eventually passed to their husbands. It therefore seems that the policy of the PAs to allocate land to *households* rather than *individuals* was, in the circumstances, a rational one.

Land Distribution: Resources

Let us now look at the process of distribution with regard to resources other than land. The legislation is silent regarding farm tools and oxen, except where it concerns peasants working under tenancy arrangements. During the initial stage of the implementation of the land reform, attempts were made, mostly by Zematcha participants in the rural areas, to confiscate landlords' oxen, implements and other property for the benefit of poorer peasants, but how successful this was, and how the confiscated property was distributed is not known.

In the first few months of the reform, when the countryside was in a volatile state, landlords took steps to dispose of their oxen as quickly as possible. Eye witness accounts tell of landlords' attempts to sell off their oxen, or slaughter them, or drive them off into hiding. One such witness, who was in western Wollega in 1976, reports that a lot of peasants were left empty-handed soon after the reform because landlords had removed their oxen from the area, some of which they drove over the border into the Sudan, and some of which they sold to slaughter-houses. According to the same source, 30% of peasant house-holders in the area had no oxen at the time of the land reform.[2]

The available evidence shows that there was a considerable shortage of farm oxen and farm implements in most parts of the country before the land reform. The severity of the shortage is indicated by the fact that in a great many rural communities, a good number of poorer peasants and tenants rented oxen for ploughing purposes.

The distribution process after 1976 did not thus concern itself with farm oxen and tools. According to our own findings, the shortage is still of serious proportions, and those without oxen in particular—the most important item of

---

[2]Ståhl, *New Seeds* ...., op.cit. pp. 39—40.

cultivation—make up a significant portion of the peasantry. Table 6 gives a breakdown of the ownership of oxen among the peasants in our interview.

Table 6. *Distribution of Farm Oxen (%)*

| Area | Number of Oxen | | | | | | |
	0	1/2*	1	2	3	4	5+
Bolloso	52	11	36	1	—	—	—
Manna	49	13	34	4	—	—	—
Adet	20	—	51	28	—	—	—
Sire	26	—	33	40	—	1	—

*This is an arrangement, not too uncommon in the two areas, whereby two (and at times, more than two) peasants own one farm animal in common.

The figures show that the shortage of oxen is most acute in Bolloso and Manna, the two areas which are at the same time the most densely populated of the four. More than half of the peasants in the first and about half in the second had no oxen at all, whereas the comparable figure for Adet and Sire is 20 and 26% respectively. Similarly, more peasants in Bolloso and Manna are short of ploughs than in the two other areas. About 40% of peasants in the former two places did not have ploughs, while only 18% in Adet and 24% in Sire were in this position. On the face of it, and insofar as the possession of oxen and tools are concerned, rural cultivators in the ensat and coffee zones are far more handicapped than those in the cereal-producing regions of the country.

The question now is how do peasants without the 'tools of their trade' manage to carry on agricultural activity and subsist? Insofar as peasants who depend on root crops for their diet (like those in Bolloso) and garden-plot cultivation (like in Manna) are concerned, to be oxen-less is not, in the last instance, a condition of dire consequence. Hand tools and backyard cultivation with the hoe will provide the peasants' food needs. For those who depend on cereal cultivation, to be without traction and traction power is a serious, but not insurmountable problem.

It will take a peasant many years and a great deal of hard work before he finally comes in possession of a pair of oxen.

In the meantime, however, he becomes dependent on friends and neighbours, who are more fortunate than himself, and with whom he strikes up a bargain for the use of their farm oxen. In Adet, the practice involves renting the animals, and payment is made through labour. The ox-less peasant here agrees to work a certain number of days on the farm of the person from whom he has rented the oxen in return for their use on his own farm. The arrangement takes a variety of forms, and depends on the agreement between ox owner and 'ox-tenant', as it were. For instance, the poor peasant may agree to work one day on the farm of the owner for every 2 days he uses the oxen on his farm. The specific terms of the agreement—which are verbal understandings and not

51

contracts—will depend on a combination of factors: the size of the poor peasant's farm, the quality of his land, his reputation as a good worker and handler of animals, the quality of the oxen, etc.

Other methods of obtaining oxen in other areas include borrowing from close relations (or friends) in which direct payment in the form of cash or labour-rent is not involved. However, the borrower, being a relation by blood or marriage, is expected to return the favour in one way or another. In some instances, poor peasants get together, pool all their resources and work each others' land in turn. Where two peasants own an ox each, the problem of joint work is made much simpler.

However, whatever arrangements are made for acquiring oxen, poor peasants' land will suffer because it will not be worked in time. Owners of oxen will make sure that their lands are ploughed and harrowed in good time before they will be willing to rent out their animals. For the dependent peasant, this might at times mean falling behind, or missing the right time for the right work.

In conclusion, redistribution—which in partial or complete form has been carried out throughout the agricultural regions of the country—has been almost exclusively restricted to farm land, and other resources were hardly involved. The few exceptions are too unimportant to mention: for example, in Manna where some small coffee processing machines, previously the property of coffee plantation owners, were taken over by PAs and are now run for the benefit of their members; in a few other places, including Bolloso and Sire, the requisitioning of storage facilities and flour mills. Of course, woodland, pasture fields, and water resources, which often were commonly used are still common property of a PA or several PAs. Peasants did not directly benefit from the nationalisation of large scale mechanised farms and their equipment, for these have become part of the government-run State Farms. That redistribution did not include the redistribution of means of cultivation, equipment and assets other than land, is because on the whole capital accumulation in the country-side was virtually nil, and the traditional, subsistence sector was considerably starved of the essential items of agricultural production.

3.3 The Results of Land Distribution

The Pattern of Holdings

At the time of our field work the land allocation in the countryside had not been completed, although its frequency was not as high as during the first three years of the land reform. In 1980/81, allocation by and large took the form of adjustment of holdings and accommodation of new (that is, young) members of Peasant Associations. However, as long as peasants continue to observe the provisions of the reform, fresh reapportionment will be carried on indefinitely, and this will affect the holding structure of rural communities. How serious the effect will be will depend on the measures taken and the local conditions which exist in each locality.

Our discussion of the distribution of holdings after land reform is based on our field work in 1980/81. Our findings, which are shown in Table 7, are not final, they only reflect conditions which prevailed at the time of our investigation in the four areas of our study. For purposes of comparison, we have also shown the distribution of holdings before the land reform.

Let us comment briefly on the results of land distribution in the four areas in our study individually.

Bolloso. The difference in the pattern of holding before and after land reform is not very significant. The overwhelming majority of holders, then as well as now, that is, 89% and 93% respectively, cultivate up to 0.5 ha of land. It is obvious from the table that a certain degree of levelling down has taken place. For example, before the land reform, holders working over 0.5 ha but less than 2 made up 11% of the total, whereas after the reform these make up 6%. At the lower end of the scale there are some changes too. Previously the smallest holders, that is, those with 0.25 ha and less made up 57% of the total, while at present they make up 51%. The change seems to be partially a result of upgrading to the next size level. Those working betwen 0.26 and 0.5 ha were 32% of the total before reform, but 42% after reform—a difference of 10%. Thus, if a certain degree of levelling down has taken place, a certain degree of levelling up has also occurred, but the over-all trend is downward.

As will be seen from the table, the majority of holders, i.e. 51%, now cultivate tiny plots, the largest of which is no bigger than 0.25 ha. To expect better yield and higher output from such petty cultivators, specially given the available technique and agricultural method, will not be realistic. In addition, modern inputs and tools cannot be easily adopted here, not only because the peasants are too poor to afford them, but also because the scale of cultivation will make such attempts largely unfruitful. In the nature of things, the great majority of Bolloso peasants will remain subsistence producers.

Manna. The size of holdings reported by peasants here is the total size of coffee as well as cereal plots. The change in the pattern of holdings in general between pre- and post-reform is more pronounced than in the case of Bolloso. To begin with, large owners, that is, those with 2.5 ha and more, who made up 8% of holders previously, have been considerably affected by the reform. Previously, those who held 2 ha and above were 13% of all holders, now they make up only 1%. More importantly, no peasant at present owns more than 2.5 ha, whereas before the reform 8% of holders worked land above this size, some of whom held plots as large as 6 hectares and above.

As Table 7 shows, the percentage of the poorest land-holding peasants, that is those working up to 0.5 ha, has decreased somewhat after the reform. At present, the majority of peasants, that is about 35%, are concentrated in the size category of between 0.51 and 0.99 ha. The result of the reform here is similar to that of Bolloso in that there has been a levelling down as well as an

Table 7 *Distribution of Land Holdings, Pre- and Post Reform (%)*

| Woreda | Period | Size in hectares | | | | | | | | | | | |
		Up to 0.25	0.26 -0.50	0.51 -0.99	1.00 -1.25	1.26 -1.50	1.51 -1.99	2.00 -2.50	2.51 -2.99	3.00 -3.99	4.00 -4.99	5.00 -5.99	6.00 and over
Bolloso	Pre-	56.65	31.65	5.50	3.44	1.83	0.69	—	—	—	—	—	—
	Post-	51.42	42.53	4.73	1.13	—	—	—	—	—	—	—	—
Manna	Pre-	15.75	29.00	15.75	15.98	6.39	3.65	5.48	—	2.51	1.60	0.91	2.74
	Post-	10.88	25.71	34.56	17.96	6.67	3.13	0.95	—	—	—	—	—
Adet	Pre-	2.58	2.35	3.99	16.90	7.75	7.51	25.59	1.88	17.14	4.68	4.46	5.16
	Post-	3.44	4.77	8.02	24.24	12.40	11.83	23.47	3.63	6.30	1.90	—	—
Sire	Pre-	2.74	10.27	45.89	14.38	10.27	6.85	4.11	2.74	0.68	—	—	2.05
	Post-	3.72	14.36	42.55	15.96	15.43	6.38	1.06	0.53	—	—	—	—

Note: Peasants gave the size of their land in local measurements which we converted into hectares. For a working system of conversion of local measurements, see C.S.O., *Results of the National Sample Survey, Second Round, Vol. V, Land Area and Utilization*, Statistical Bulletin 10, Addis Ababa, February 1975.

up-grading, although in the case of Manna, the levelling down is greater in magnitude. In Bolloso, the great majority of peasants hold up to 0.5 ha of land, but in Manna only 37% of them are in this position.

Adet. The distribution of holdings after land reform is different here and to some extent far more even than in all our research areas. This is partly because landlessness was not an acute problem previously (although it did exist) since Adet was in the rist system, and partly because holdings were not as diminutive, on average, as in the other areas. While there is some degree of levelling down here too, the magnitude is much smaller. There is, too, some measure of up-grading, but not among the poorer peasants but among those in the 'middle' category. Previously, about 9% of peasants held less than 1 ha each, but the figure now is about 16%. Those holding between 1 and 2.5 ha made up 58% of holders before the reform, but 72% after the reform. Then, as now, the majority of holdings are in this category. Before reform, 28% of holders held land over 2.5 ha but under 6 ha; at present, only 12% are in this position.

Sire. The result of distribution of holdings here is similar to that in Manna; there has been some down-grading at the top end, some up-grading at the bottom. Then, as well as now, the majority of holdings—i.e. 46% and 42% respectively—are over 0.5 but under 1 ha. Those who cultivated between 1 and 1.5 ha were 24% of the total previously, but 31% now. At present, about 60% of all peasants cultivate holdings below 1 ha, and about 40% between 1 and 1.5 ha.

In conclusion, land distribution has not brought about significant changes in the status of a majority of peasants in terms of *size* of holdings; as the table above shows, the pattern of distribution of land before and after reform is not markedly different. This is not at all surprising because what was redistributed was what was already under cultivation by the peasants themselves. Indeed, in the allocation process, landless peasants were included, which meant that the available land was shared among a greater number of peasants than before. In consequence, a significant majority of holders in all the areas of our research are mini-plot cultivators and, except in Adet, the great portion of them work less than 1 hectare of land each.[1]

One problem, which was, previously, a major cause for inefficiency and waste in peasant production, was *fragmentation* of plots. In many parts of the country, peasants worked not consolidated plots, but parcels scattered over a fairly large area, and quite a distance from the homestead.

Our investigation attempted to determine the extent to which fragmentation had been dealt with in the process of implementation of the reform. We discovered that by and large the problem was still serious, that it was in fact not taken into account during land distribution, and that in some instances it has

---

[1]The results of Tesfaye Teclu's studies of land reform in 3 woredas in 1977–78 correspond with our findings. See his *Socio-Economic Conditions in Shashemene, Doddota, and Danglla, 1978.* IDR Research Report Nos. 26, 27, 28, Addis Ababa, Institute of Development Research, 1979.

been aggravated. The reason for this had to do with the manner in which distribution was carried out.

In an attempt to be fair and just to all, PAs distributed plots in parcels of different quality and location. Each household which received land was given pieces, rather than a consolidated piece, from the different categories of land in the land fund, so that the final allotment consisted of two or more parcels located in different parts of the community. Some households which were large in size ended up with large numbers of parcels—as many as 8 or 10—because each member of the household's share consisted of more than one parcel. Plot consolidation was not a goal in many PAs, the goal rather was equity as conceived by the peasants.

The best result in terms of minimisation of fragmentation after land reform was found in Sire woreda, where, it will be recalled, PAs had made great efforts to discourage holdings which were fragmented or far away from peasant dwellings. Here, half of the peasants in our survey used to work two or more parcels before, whereas after land distribution, only 26% were in this position. The great majority of holdings, that is 74%, were single plots. At the opposite extreme was Manna, where parcellisation had become worse than before. Previously over half of the holders cultivated consolidated plots, but after land reform the figure had dropped to 31%. In addition, the percentage of holders working 2 and more plots had also increased. The situation in Bolloso and Adet falls in between these two extremes. On the whole, the problem here had not been either dramatically improved or similarly worsened. There is some worsening of the situation in both cases. In Adet in particular, the problem is of serious magnitude: at present, more than half the peasants work four or more parcels individually.

The Beneficiaries of Land Distribution

Land reform is not only concerned with the redistribution of wealth, but also brings about changes in the class composition of rural society, although this will depend on the content of the reform and the manner of its implementation. Serious studies of the class structure of rural Ethiopia before the reform are few and these are not quite exhaustive. Official documents which contain general surveys of the countryside and published during the 1960s talk in terms of landowners and tenants, but do not sufficiently distinguish between small and large owners, between land held by the aristrocracy and that held by small or medium holders, etc., and therefore are of limited value for assessing the class structure of the rural population. It is known, though not precisely, that rural society contained social elements other than owners and tenants, that landless peasants (and we believe that any rural resident marginally involved in agricultural activity, however destitute, must be called a peasant in the Ethiopian context), hired labourers, small owners as well as medium landlords were part of the agrarian community. The class composition of each locality of course

Table 8. *Social Status and Peasants before Reform*

	1 Total	2 Landlord	3 Owner- culti- vator	4 Tenant	5 Wage	6 Landless	7 Mixed 3+4	8 Other
Bolloso	531(100)	1(0)	325(61)	107(20)	—	33(6)	5(1)	65(12)
Manna	735(100)	8(1)	124(17)	268(36)	87(12)	33(4)	36(5)	179(24)
Adet	524(100)	25(5)	157(30)	75(14)	—	20(4)	169(32)	78(15)
Sire	188(100)	4(2)	19(10)	116(62)	—	9(5)	5(3)	35(19)

Note: Figures in brackets are %. Col. 5 refers to hired farm labourers. Col. 8 includes those who were minors before the reform, urban residents, etc.

differs from others, nevertheless, social analysis which restricts itself to the interaction between owner and tenant alone will be incomplete.

To determine the class content of the communities we surveyed, we asked peasants to describe their status before the reform. The result appears in Table 8.

As the table shows, the percentage of landlords is quite small. We are here talking about small landlords, who owned up to 10 hectares of land, who themselves engaged in farming but leased some of their possessions to others in return for rent. The aristocracy and the landed local gentry are not included because they were not physically present in the countryside, that is, they did not themselves engage in rural production.

Owner-cultivators, that is, those who owned and cultivated their own plots, who, at least legally, were independent producers, were an important element of rural society prior to 1975. In Bolloso, the majority, and in Adet about a third (if we ignore mixed cultivators in column 7 of Table 8), of peasants fell in this category. What will be the attitude of peasants of this sort to land reform, and how will they be affected by land distribution? Of all the class of peasants identified above, owner-cultivators will be the ones who will harbour an ambivalent attitude to land reform or may benefit the least from it. We shall return to this point later.

According to our findings, the extent of tenancy varied considerably from one area to another. It was very high in Sire, about 62% of all peasants, but low in Adet and Bolloso. As far as the size of landless peasants is concerned, it ranged from 6% in Bolloso (the highest) to less than 48% in Adet (the lowest).

Let us now try to evaluate the effect of land distribution—and indeed, the reform in general—on the various social groups within the peasant world. The reform has not been equally beneficial to all sectors of rural society; while many have gained, many others who should have been beneficiaries, have lost. One thing, however, is commonly and equally shared by all, namely that all rural producers have usufructuary rights over the land they cultivate and private ownership has been done away with. The owner-cultivator as well as the tenant or landless peasant have been reduced to the same status in this regard.

Who has benefited and who has lost?

A closer examination of the effect of the reform on the various social elements in Ethiopia's rural society shows that the benefit is not of equal weight, is not evenly distributed in all cases. Those who lost outright can of course be easily identified: they were the landed classes whose property was confiscated and whose economic and political power was thoroughly broken. If we turn to the beneficiaries themselves we observe that the net effect has been uneven.

Of all peasants, those who benefitted most are the landless. All things being equal, as the economists say, a peasant is much better off with a piece of land than without however small the size of the plot may be. It would be too involved to determine the amount of land the landless managed to acquire in all of our woredas, but it is safe to suggest that their holdings are among the smaller of the lot.

The second category of peasants who have clearly benefitted are former tenants, and their gain is not so much in terms of size of holdings acquired, as in the removal of burdens imposed on them by the previous tenurial arrangement. According to our study, 82% of former tenants in Sire, and 69% in Manna used to give up a quarter and a half of their harvest respectively in the form of rent before the reform. The size of former tenants varies considerably from one area to another, being as high as 62% in Sire, and as low as 14% in Adet.

Land reform has had mixed results for that class of peasants who formerly were owner-cultivators, i.e., those who owned and personally cultivated small plots of land. Some have gained, i.e., the plots they are now cultivating are larger than before; some have lost, and some have remained with the same size of land as formerly. Whether or not the land that owner-cultivators is now holding is of better or poorer quality cannot be fully ascertained, although in most cases peasants of this kind are still in possession of their former plots. If we compare the size of holdings of owner-cultivators before and after the land reform in Bolloso and Adet, where peasants of this kind were numerous, we obtain the result shown in Table 9.

A majority of owner-cultivators in Adet, i.e., 66%, hade been not losers, whereas in Bolloso the corresponding figure is 17%. The experience of Sire is similar to that of Adet in this regard, although the percentage of those who lost is not as high, and owner-cultivators were only 10% of the total population.

Land Distribution and Rural Differentiation

If we look at the distribution of holdings shown in Table 7 above, we note that holdings are not equal and that some peasants have more land than others. The question now is: has the land reform given rise to a new form of social

Table 9. *Owner-cultivators' Holdings Before and After Reform. Percentage of Peasants with Holdings*

	Larger than before	Smaller	Unchanged
Bolloso	31	17	51
Adet	17	66	17

stratification among the peasantry, and can we talk in terms of poor peasants, and well-off peasants or Kulaks? In order to answer this question, we need first to determine how to identify social classes within the peasant community. Some have argued that such an exercise is altogether futile since peasant communities are by and large homogenous, and that if differences exist they are a result of demographic factors rather than social ones. A.V. Chayanov, and more recently, T. Shanin, have argued along this line in respect of the Russian peasantry of the pre-revolution period. In contrast, the debate among party leaders in the Soviet Union in the 1920s raised a number of issues with regard to the analysis of classes and social polarisation within the peasantry.

In discussing Russian agriculture at the turn of the century, Lenin argued that differentiation among the peasantry was taking place at a rapid rate, and the old patriarchal peasant would eventually disappear from the rural scene. He saw this process of differentiation as an indication of the emergence of capitalism and commodity production in agriculture. He singled out what he called the rural bourgeoisie—i.e. the well-off peasant who was engaged in commercial agriculture in all its forms—and the rural proletariat as the main forces of rural capitalism. The differentiation of the peasantry, Lenin believed, was taking place at the expense of the 'middle peasantry' who stood in between the well-to-do and the destitute classes, and who was unable to evolve into a commodity producer.[2] What is important is that Lenin identified rural classes not in terms of size of land holdings, but in terms of the nature of the individuals' productive activity and their relations to the means of production. The rural bourgeois was a bourgeois not because he had large holdings, but because he was engaged in the main in commodity production.

Lenin characterised the process of differentiation as 'de-peasantisation', and noted that this involved the dissolution of the old peasantry, and the emergence of new rural classes associated with commodity production.[3] The dissolution of the old peasantry—either through de-peasantisation or other ways—was for

[2]Lenin: *The Development of Capitalism in Russia*, 1907 edn., (Moscow, Progress Publishers, 1964), pp. 174–185.
[3]Ibid., p. 184.

him inevitable, and desirable if rural production was to be freed from all the fetters that retarded its development.

Another experience which has some relevance to our own case is the Egyptian agrarian reform of 1952–1970. In these years, land reform was carried out three times, and the chief aim in all cases was to eliminate imbalances, and to reduce inequalities among the rural population. Many observers of the Egyptian experience, however, contend that the reforms did not do away with class diffcrences within the peasantry and, on the contrary, they have clearly favoured the class of rich and middle peasants. One Egyptian writer, who has made a study of the process of agrarian transition in the country, has argued that the analysis of the class structure of rural Egypt must be based not on the size of peasant holdings, but on the level of wage employment, the degree of farm mechanisation, and the extent of crop specialisation, i.e. whether cash crops or subsistence crops are raised. He identifies five rural classes on the basis of these criteria, and the most prosperous classes—those he calls middle and rich peasantry—are those who hire wage labour, whose farms use better technology, and who tend to specialise in commercially high-valued crops such as fruit and vegetables. He estimates that something like 71% of the total wage labour of the country is employed by middle and rich peasants.[4]

These two examples will suffice to illustrate the point we wish to make. In both the Russian and Egyptian experiences cited, differentiation among peasants is a qualitative one, that is, the factors that are identified have a bearing on the quality of agricultural performance. Central in both arguments is that those considered prosperous classes are distinguished from others because: 1. They employ wage labour; 2. They use modern equipment and inputs (or at least, their equipment and inputs are relatively superior to those of the average peasant); and 3. The market plays an important role in their productive plans, though not all of them produce *exclusively* for the market. These same factors have been used to distinguish classes in other agrarian conditions, both before and after reform.

If we employ these criteria, especially the first two, to rural conditions in Post-reform Ethiopia, we will have to conclude that the reform has not created class distinctions within rural society. The differences in size of holdings, noted in our discussion earlier, cannot justify the view that land reform has given rise to class distinctions within the peasantry. The distribution process in a large number of PAs in our study—as indeed throughout the country—was based on family size, and previous social and holding status. The reform itself has closed virtually all avenues by which enterprising peasants, or 'capitalist-roaders', could separate from the peasantry and emerge as rich peasants, kulaks or rural bourgeoisie.

There is a more important reason why differences in holdings should not be

---

[4]M. Abdel-Fadil, *Development, Income Distribution and Social Change in Rural Egypt (1952–70). A Study in the Political Economy of Agrarian Transition,* (Cambridge University Press, 1975), p. 28.

taken as qualitative, class, or protoclass differences. The peasant with 3 hectares of land, for instance, is only slightly better-off than the one with 1 hectare, for the reason that both are fettered by the same 'mode' of production. They use the same traditional implements, the same cultivation methods, and the object of production in both is identical, namely, self-sustenance. Those with larger plots cannot reap the benefits since they cannot hire labour, or rent out parts of their land to others. The law requires that land be given to those who are willing to engage in personal cultivation. True, peasants with bigger plots, who also have large families of working age and surplus oxen may be in a good position to produce more, but much of the produce will be used up at home to feed the family. It is, however, unlikely that this kind of fortuitous combination exists in many communities and, indeed, as we saw in the previous section, very few peasants in our survey own more than a pair of oxen.

The initial impact of Ethiopa's agrarian reform, especially but not exclusively in areas of high population density and shortage of land, has been in the direction of peasantisation, that is, the creation of small cultivators, undifferentiated, therefore uncompetitive, insecure in terms of meeting their basic needs, and unable to be involved in initiatives towards improvement and modernisation of their farms.

Of course, the differences in size of holdings cannot be ignored as being altogether inconsequential. A great majority of peasants in all our areas, except Adet, hold land below 1 hectare, and a small percentage over 2 hectares; in Adet a small group holds between 3 and 5 hectares. The difference between the peasant with, say 4 hectares, and another with 0.25 hectares, cannot be dismissed as insignificant. We must also note that quite a large portion of peasants do not possess oxen and ploughs. Those with small plots, but more importantly without the basic means of cultivation, are at a distinct disadvantage in comparison with those better endowed. We can therefore talk in terms of *quantitative* differentiation between *poor* peasants (or lower peasantry) and *self-sufficing* peasants (or upper peasantry). Poor peasants are those who have plots which by the standards of their community are small and, in addition, do not own the basic means of cultivation. For instance, in ensat areas, this would include owners of up to 0.5 ha of land, and in the cereal growing areas those with up to 1.5 hectares at the least.

The difference between the lower and upper peasantry is however a difference in relation to the ability to meet one's family needs, and not in relation to better marketable surplus production, or the accumulation of capital. The poor peasant will be hard put to meet his subsistence requirements, and indeed is often fairly destitute, but his opposite number is in a relatively better position. But the margin of difference, in *qualitative* terms, particularly with regard to accumulation, is insignificant.

The land reform has ruled out the possibility of the emergence of a kulak class in the countryside. Furthermore, so long as the agrarian law now in force remains unchanged, so long, that is, the right to land use is encumbent on membership in PAs, whose available land is fixed and unchangeable, so long will the levelling down process continue, and differences in size of holdings, which now appear significant, will gradually disappear. This *dynamic* process will lead to what we wish to call *agrarian involution*, that is, a tendency, already in evidence, of peasants turning inwards, of being concerned solely with self-sustenance rather than involvement in the general exchange process, in accumulation in innovative endeavour.

In conclusion, the land reform has substantially modified the social profile of rural Ethiopia. Not only has tenancy as well as landlordism been abolished, but landlessness has been greatly minimised. In terms of the relationship of the producer to his means of production, all differences have been eliminated, and each peasant now holds usufruct rights over the land he employs for his livelihood. In this sense, rural society can be said to have been 'de-stratified', and inequalities based on the right to labour have been abolished. Furthermore, by transforming all rural producers into usufructuary holders of land, the reform has also created a *uniformity of tenure*, and of *social conditions*, in rural society.

3.4 Land Reform and After

Introduction

The transition from one agrarian system to another, particularly under conditions of social and economic backwardness, cannot be completed within a short span of time. It is a process, and therefore, the emerging system will unfold itself over a period of many years. Needless to say, the completion of the transition will be more *or* less successful, more *or* less rapid, depending on the prevalence of a conducive political atmosphere, and on the kind of encouragement and incentive provided to the countryside by state and local authorities.

At the time of our investigation, the institutional framework of the new agrarian order was already in evidence. The landlord had disappeared from the rural scene, individual possessions had been clearly defined, and Peasant Associations had become a permanent feature of the peasant community.

Elias Tuma has argued that there are, broadly speaking, two types of agrarian reform. The first is within the framework of private property, and calls for individuals holdings, small, family-operated farms, and allows a certain degree of inequality of wealth and income. The second type involves the nationalisation of land, and thereby the abolition of private ownership in land; it favours large-scale farming and stresses the elimination of class differences based on land. This typology is quite narrow, and in any event the Ethiopian experience does not fit into any of the two categories. Essentially, the country's reform is a distributive one, though within the context of land nationalisation–

–but a distributive reform accompanied by a levelling effect[1] as was discussed earlier. The reform may in short be described as a distributive-levelling reform based on a fixed but increasingly diminishing rural asset.

Had the reform been accompanied by such schemes as colonisation of new land, bringing unused land into cultivation and, of course, growth in industry and commerce, it would have been a distributive-expansive reform, in that the sources of rural wealth would be increasingly enlarged. As it is, the pressure on the land will continue to grow, and the size of the average family farm will become smaller.

This is the more so in that on top of the factors already discussed, the reform has had a considerable impact, at least *initially,* on the magnitude of rural to urban migration. We were unable to obtain hard data on migration, for it would have involved conducting a survey of some of the major towns in our areas—a task which was beyond our means. But from our discussions with peasants, peasant leaders and local government officials we were able to gather that to a certain extent the reform has discouraged peasant migration to the urban areas. The reasons for this are not hard to fathom.

1. A peasant's land, and his right to its use, depends on his continued residence in a rural community, and membership in the PA of that community. If he is away for an extended period of time, he may forfeit his right to the land. Most rural migrants do not wish to break their ties to their homeland, and this is a barrier to migration.

2. Although no adequate studies are available, it is safe to presume that many of the rural migrants before the land reform were landless peasants.[2] Now that the landless have benefitted by the reform, the reason for migration is not as strong as before.

3. The towns are no longer as attractive in terms of employment, housing, etc. for peasants as previously.

It is not only rural to urban migration that has been reduced, but inter-rural migration as well, and for similar reasons. The decrease in rural-to-urban migration has a positive as well as a negative side to it: positive because the urban areas will be relieved of the pressure of high unemployment and its accompanying social consequences, negative because as far as the rural communities are concerned, the pressure on the land will be greatly intensified. *In the long run, therefore, peasant migration will be accelerated by the land reform itself.*

---

[1]Elias H. Tuma, *Twenty-six Centuries of Agrarian Reform: A Comparative Analysis,* (Berkeley, University of California Press, 1965), chapter XIV. More recently, D. Lehmann has argued that all contemporary ideologies of land reform are either "historicist" or "technocratic"; however, Ethiopia's reform ideology does not fit into either of these two categories. See 'The Death of Land Reform: A Polemic,' *World Development,* vol. 6, No. 3, 1978.

The term 'distributive' is used in the sense suggested by Michael Lipton, 'Towards a theory of Land Reform', in D. Lehmann (ed) *Agrarian Reform and Agrarian Reformism* (London, Faber and Faber, 1974).

[2]See my own *Awassa: A Limited Impact Study* (A Social Survey of a Provincial Town), Institute of Development Research, Report No. 29, Addis Ababa, 1979.

Land Reform and Rural Technology

It has been argued by some that land reform does not immediately result in rapid technical change in rural production; for this to happen, a concerted effort on the part of state and local authorities to provide technical advice, new equipment, credit and needed services must be made.[3] All peasants in all the areas we covered were using the same traditional farm implements, and the same age-old methods of cultivation. In Bolloso, where the locally based rural development agency, WADU, had made some effort to introduce improved ways of farming, peasants were as traditional as their counter-parts in other areas.

On the other hand, it would be expected that once peasants are freed from dependence and obligations to landlords, once, that is, they become independent producers, they will show greater interest in innovations for the purpose of improving their production. This is in fact one of the important arguments in favour of land reform. Peasant attitude to technical change may also be positively affected if improved means of cultivation are made easily available and at prices which they can afford. At present, the enterprising peasant who may be willing to experiment with new ideas is as traditional as his opposite counterpart for the reason that the technology is not accessible to him. This is in fact a serious and long-term problem, for the country does not have industries that produce modern farm equipment worthy of the name, and the kind of cheap and effective tools needed for Ethiopia's rural conditions may not be easily available elsewhere.

In any event, we found no evidence that as a result of land reform peasants had developed a heightened awareness of the need for technical innovations and improved methods of farming. This is quite understandable, for to create the need for innovations, peasants must be exposed to them, and the effectiveness of the new ideas clearly demonstrated. The level of technical knowledge in the countryside, that is, traditional craft knowledge, is so low, and the quality of craft products so poor that *innovative ideas will not emerge from within the peasantry itself but must be introduced from outside.*

Most of the implements employed by the peasant are locally made. The peasant's reliance on the world outside his community is just as limited in this regard as in his other needs. The rural blacksmith who makes the metal portions of farm tools, and the peasant himself who makes the other parts, together satisfy almost all the technological needs of the rural community. The cash value of the entire array of farm equipment needed by the average present—namely the plough, the sickle, a few varieties of hand tools, the wooden winnower—adds up, maximally, to about 20 US dollars.

---

[3]For a study of the complex problems involved in the diffusion of agricultural innovations in one rural setting in Ethiopia, see I. Jonsson, *Diffusion of Agricultural Innovations in Chillalo Awraja, Ethiopia*, IDR Research Report No. 17, Addis Ababa, June 1975.

In so far as fertilisers and improved seeds are concerned, peasant attitude in favour of using them is changing gradually. It appears that many peasants are aware of the usefulness of these inputs, although a majority do not still use them, either because they are too costly or because they are not easily available. Those who have tried using them, particularly chemical fertilisers, have done so only for a limited number of seasons. The price of fertilisers for peasants has gone up quite considerably within the last three to four years, and this has acted as a brake on their wider distribution.

The woreda-level extension services do not as a rule offer financial credit to peasants, the only exception being WADU in Bolloso, which for a time provided credit to peasants but which has discontinued the service now. Peasants in need, therefore turn to relatives and friends to obtain loans, and sometimes to borrow grain or seeds.

It is interesting to note that the land reform has done away with the local money-lender. Previously the money-lender was often an urban resident—a small business man, an official, or a landlord—and advanced money to peasants at exorbitant rates of interest. The defaulting peasant was in serious trouble, for the money man, who often had good connections with law-enforcing agents, would have the peasants harvest or his livestock impounded. Peasants who were unable to pay on time took out more loans, either from the same person, or another, to cover their previous debts, thus falling in the process further into debt.

The land reform has done away with all that, but has not created an alternative mechanism to cater for the needs of peasants. The PA would have been the best alternative in this regard, but, as we shall see later, most PAs are in no position to provide credit or manage services of this sort.

Peasants at present borrow money from other peasants, relatives, etc., and virtually no interest is involved*. In our survey, the proportion of peasants who had borrowed money recently varied from 69% in Bolloso to 9% in Sire; about 19% and 17% of peasants in Manna and Adet respectively had similarly borrowed money. The extent of borrowing—even if from fellow peasants—is exceptionally high in Bolloso. On the whole, the level of borrowing has not markedly changed in any of the areas from before the land reform.

The amount of money borrowed by peasants is often very small, between 30 and 50 Birr (15 to 25 US dollars), and the purpose is usually to purchase small items for personal consumption, foods, seeds, and to pay taxes: at times however, the loan is used to acquire agricultural necessities. Where the loan is meant for the latter purpose, in particular for acquiring livestock, the size of the loan is fairly large. One source of expense for which a large number of peasants sought credit is the traditional 'digis'—a feasts in connection with weddings, christenings, religious holidays, etc.

---

*There is some evidence that in a few areas peasants themselves (those that also double-up as rural traders) are stepping into the shoes of the old money-lender.

Agricultural Prices and Taxation

Our survey of the general conditions of peasants after land reform will not be complete without some discussion concerning agricultural prices, and peasant involvement in the exchange process. There is a consensus among students of agrarian reform that for reform to be successful, and to set in motion the forces of development, rural production must be firmly and securely integrated into the general exchange process. However, the attempt to do so, and to thereby create a single, inter-dependent national economy has, according to Hyden, failed in many African countries, both in those who have had agrarian reform and those who have not. The African peasantry has resisted 'capture' by the state or urban social forces, and continues its traditional and autonomous form of existence, despite efforts in the opposite direction by planners and policy-makers.[4] If agrarian reform is to break this experience and create the conditions for a vigorous economy, it must begin to meet the needs of the peasantry and to satisfy its interests.

There is no tried and true formula for bringing this about, but many argue that a system combining attractive prices for agricultural goods, better market-ing services, and inducements towards greater reliance on exchange will be a step further. This is, of course, suggested in the context of private peasant production. The transformation of peasant production—the major goal of agrarian reform—will occur if the *market acts as a productive force,* and the chief purpose of production becomes exchange rather than self-sustenance.

Since 1977, the government has fixed prices of agricultural goods, and at the local level, peasants must sell their produce at the official rates. Free market prices are of course higher, but a number of control mechanisms have been put in force to ensure that peasants do not sell except at the prices set by the government. One method is that peasants are required to deliver, through their PAs, a fixed quota of agricultural produce to the state marketing corporation which pays at the official rates. A second method is that consumers can only buy grain from their local urban kebbeles and not directly from the peasants; the kebbeles in the smaller towns purchase their stock from peasants at the official rates, in others they obtain them through the marketing corporation. For instance, in the woreda town of Adet, peasants were offered 41 Birr for a quintal of high grade teff, 25 Birr per quintal for barley, and 17 Birr per quintal for maize in 1981. Prices were set not only for cereals, but for cash crops such as coffee, chat and oil seeds.

The government's prime motive in fixing prices may have been to hold down food prices in the urban areas, but, be that as it may, the price system for agriculture has not been favourably received by a large number of peasants. Without a comparable policy with regard to manufactures and other items of

---

[4]Goran Hyden, *Beyond Ujamaa in Tanzania, Underdevelopment and an Uncaptured Peasantry* (Berkeley, Univ. Calif. Press 1980), pp. 32—33.

peasant's consumption it will be difficult to expect peasants to be well disposed to what is offered to them for their produce. Peasants in Adet, for instance, felt particularly resentful of the unfavourable price structure, and for comparison they pointed to a long list of goods whose prices had gone up sharply within the last five years. Among the items were such essentials as salt, which according to the peasants, had gone up by 75%, paraffin, by over 200%, etc.: even local craft products such as leather goods and clothes had nearly trebled in price in their estimation. Whether or not peasants were accurate in their view that prices of many manufactures and other items at the village market have risen sharply is not the main point: the main point is the growing conviction among peasants that they are not offered commensurate prices for their products.

Now, the main concern here is not just that peasants are unhappy about the price policy in force, but the repercussions that this will have on rural production. If peasants had no option but to sell their goods at whatever prices, i.e. if they were dependent on the market system as well as on the national economy, a price structure unfavourable to them might be tolerated for a while. Peasants, however, do have an option: they can hold back their surplus from the market at any time. This problem is of particular concern to the country because, now as well as before the reform, Ethiopia remains a country of subsistence agriculture. A greater portion of the rural produce—82% as recently estimated by CSO—does not appear in the market but is consumed by the producers themselves.

Mention also must be made about the agricultural tax system instituted after land reform. Previously, the tax structure was quite complicated, and peasants had to pay not only taxes related to agricultural activities, but also taxes for social services such as education and health, although the countryside benefitted the least from these services. Tax assessments were made on what was produced, as well as on such factors as the size and quality of land, the system of tenure involved and the region where the land was located.[5]

The new tax system has greatly simplified matters; it has done away with all taxes except those related to agricultural activities, and has adopted a uniform method of assessment. At present, all peasants pay what is called a land use fee which, for all individual cultivators irrespective of size of holdings or quality of land, is set at 10 Birr per year. They also pay an agricultural income tax, which is assessed at a graduated rate based on the annual income of each cultivator, with the minimum set at 10 Birr. For almost all peasants, the total tax payment comes to 20 Birr per year.[6] The new tax system has one drawback: it does not make allowances for inequalities of holdings, differences in the quality of land, and the mini-holder as well as the large holder are made to pay the same amount. Consequently, some peasants, particularly the poorer ones, complain that it is unfair, that it in effect discriminates against small peasants.

---

[5]See the *Consolidated Laws of Ethiopia,* vol. I, Addis Ababa, Faculty of Law, 1972, for details.
[6]PMAC, *Negarit Gazeta,* Proc. No. 77, 1976, and amended by Proc. No. 152, 1978.

A few words about an activity in which virtually all peasants were involved and which was quite common throughout the countryside at the time of our field work. For a number of years after land reform, peasants were required to make payments to a wide variety of what were known as public fund-raising campaigns. Although participation in this effort was voluntary, the campaigns themselves were actively supported by officials of local government, and peasants had little choice but to be involved. Payment was often in cash, but on occasions payment in kind or even in labour was accepted. Among the most important of these fund-raising activities were those in support of victims of drought and famine, in support of the 1977—78 war, and later, to assist victims of the war, and for the rural literacy campaign. In addition, peasants were responsible for building a number of common-purpose facilities in their woreda, such as offices for the various rural organisations, assembly halls, sports fields or public squares in the woreda town, etc. On top of all this, peasants also had to pay their annual membership fees to the PA and to the youth and women's associations.

Although some of the payments were small enough not to be a serious strain on peasant income, the cumulative effect of these recurrent campaigns was such that many peasants felt over-burdened and resentful.

Rural Conditions After Reform: Prospects

We now come to the general question of how far the standard of living of the peasant community has improved and to what extent rural conditions have been positively affected. Economic indicators related to standard of living, levels of income and consumption for the farming community are not available, and therefore our discussion of these questions is based on our own impressions and observations.

Generally speaking, the effect of the land reform on income and pattern of consumption is not reflected in clear and visible outward forms, that is, in better clothing, new and improved farm equipment, new and better-built housing, etc. Peasants in Bolloso and Manna are, relatively, better dressed than those in Adet and Sire, but this is not a result of differences in income but rather a reflection of differences in custom and social attitudes. For the most part, peasant homes in all regions are built in the same traditional way, and the difference between the poor and the better-off is not readily apparent in this regard.

Doreen Warriner contends that whether or not land reform has been a success is determined, initially, by whether or not peasants eat better than before reform.[7] To accurately establish how far the peasants' diet has improved is a rather complicated and time-consuming task. It seems reasonable to expect

---

[7]*Land Reform in Principle and in Practice* (Oxford, Clarendon Press, 1969), p. 29.

however, that with land reform, with the abolition of peasant exploitation by the landed classes, the rural population would be better placed to improve its food consumption, both in quantity and quality. Many peasants will therefore now eat more and better than before, and this is borne out by the answers we got to our questions on the issue. We asked peasants if they were feeding better now than before reform. Slightly over half of our respondents in Bolloso and Manna answered in the affirmative, while in Adet and Sire, the figure was a little more than a third, with an equal proportion answering that their diet has remained unchanged. Food shortages, however, have continued to plague the urban population, and the extent of famine-affected areas has, according to official sources, continued to grow in the last five years.

The PA cooperative shops, which are now common throughout the country-side, offer a variety of goods to peasants at better prices than the open market. The shops were reasonably well-stocked and compared well with medium-sized shops in the bigger provincial towns. Both in the co-op shops and in the open market, the variety of goods offered to peasants has not, however, changed since land reform. In all the regions in our study, what was available was standard rural-oriented goods such as salt, cloth, yarn, paraffin and cooking oil, sewing items, and the like. High quality and durable goods are unknown. It is clear from this that the pattern of consumption of the peasantry has not really changed significantly, and the notion of the peasant who is claimed to have become accustomed to high levels of consumption and who is demanding high quality and expensive merchandise is obviously a gross exaggeration.

For at great majority of peasants in our study—and this holds true for other areas as well—farm work, that is crop production and livestock raising, remains the only source of income. However, farming activity, even where there are two harvest seasons in the year, which is the case in many places, does not fully occupy peasants throughout the year, and outside of the peak seasons, the average peasant stays idle or only marginally occupied. Studies about work––its volume, intensity and duration—in rural communities are not readily available. Nevertheless, it is generally accepted that peasants spend part of the work-year doing nothing, and another part of it in carrying on non-economic activities. One short survey shows, for example, that peasants remain idle for about 14% of the work-year, and another 23% of the year is devoted to the observation of religious holidays and involvement in traditional social functions. This means that about one-third of the labour time of peasants is devoted to non-productive work, that only two-thirds of the work year is economically utilised.[8]

In the slack seasons, peasants may engage in activities directly related to farming, such as making replacements of necessary equipment, repairing tools, dwellings, etc.; these are essential, but do not earn them any supplementary

---

[8]Fassil G. Kiros, 'Estimates of the Proportion of the Potential Work Year Allocated to Socio-Cultural Functions in Rural Ethiopia', *Ethiopian Journal of Development Research*, vol. 2. no. 2, 1976.

income. Supplementary sources of income, and especially outside agriculture, are quite limited, and the enterprising peasant who may wish to earn more by side-line employment has few opportunities of doing so. No new opportunities have been created for the rural population in this regard by the land reform. For the most part, supplementary employment is possible only in traditional handicraft and petty trading.

Except in Bolloso, the number of peasants engaged in income-earning side-line employment was not very high: 21% peasants in Sire, 12% in Adet and 10% in Manna. The types of employment resorted to by those with side-line occupations is shown in Table 10. In Bolloso, however, about 43% of peasants in our interview were involved in non-farm occupation, a majority of whom (about 65%) in petty trading. This might be taken as an indication that peasants here are more destitute than others, and that they have a greater need to supplement their income. This is only partly true, however, as Bolloso peasants, or Wollaita peasants in general, have long been involved in trading activities, and the practice of combining farming with itinerant peddling has a long history in this region. The reasons for this may be economic, but it has also been reinforced by the prevailing agricultural system of the area. The cultivation of ensat, and other long-maturing tuberous crops does not require as much attention as the cultivation of cereals, and therefore peasants in the ensat zone—like those in Bolloso—can afford to be engaged in other activities and to be away from their farms for extended periods of time. In their absence, their farms are looked after by their wives and the younger members of the household.

That some peasants in Adet and Sire earn income as hired labourers is due to fortuitous circumstances; in the former case, it is because of a major road-building project in the area, and in the latter, the existence of a medium-sized mechanised farm close to the woreda town. In Manna, on the other hand, some peasants hire themselves out during the coffee-picking season, and although such form of agricultural labour is prohibited by the reform, PAs in the area, as also in other coffee-growing regions do not actively discourage it.

Although the lack of reliable data on the standard of life of peasants and their level of income makes it difficult to determine accurately the effect of the reform, it can nevertheless be said that in terms of wealth and income, the status of a great number of peasants has not markedly changed. As we tried to show earlier, those who benefitted most were former tenants and the landless. The strength of the reform lies not so much in having enlarged the resources or the accumulated wealth of the rural community as in having created equal opportunities for all. By equal opportunities we mean the guarantee of land, however small it may be, to each peasant through his rural organisation. The performance of the rural economy will be dependent therefore on the system of holdings that has been established by the reform, a system in which each peasant is an independent producer and enjoys usufruct rights over his land.

In the long run, the new land system will enable peasants to meet their basic needs better than the old system, and the consumption of many of them may

Table 10. *Types of Occupation Engaged in*

		1	2	3	4	5	6	7	8	Total*
Bolloso	No	5	31	4	25	6	171	5	17	264
	%	2	12	2	9	2	65	2	6	100
Manna	No	—	2	—	15	9	12	15	23	76
	%	—	3	—	20	12	16	20	30	101
Adet	No	13	—	6	4	—	9	2	28	62
	%	21	—	10	6	—	15	3	45	100
Sire	No	18	—	—	9	—	3	6	3	39
	%	46	—	—	23	—	8	15	8	100

* Respondents could give more than one answer.

Note: 1=Weaving; 2=Pottery; 3=Leatherwork; 4=Woodwork and tool making; 5=Building work (traditional); 6=Trade; 7=Wage labour; 8=Other work.

improve to some extent. However, improvement of peasant's primary needs, a desirable aim in itself, cannot be the sole purpose of agrarian reform, but that together with this it must stimulate rural production, and encourage an increasing amount of the agricultural surplus to be released for development purposes. Without an effective system of incentives, such as a reasonable price policy, and ancillary support, such as credit and marketing services, cheaper inputs, etc.—which at present arc lacking, or inadequate—it is hard to envisage an appreciable and sustained growth in peasant production. Indeed, the new land system, in conjunction with the agricultural policies now in force, has had the undesirable effect of making peasants turn inwards, that is, concentrate their efforts in satisfying their own needs, rather than being actively involved in the exchange process.

The Emerging Agrarian Structure

By way of conclusion, we would like to make a few points on the emerging agrarian structure of the country, and on the performance of rural production since land reform. It may be noted at the outset that no definitive conclusion can be made at this point on both questions, since on the one hand changes are still taking place in the countryside, and on the other, data on many aspects of rural production are either unavailable or incomplete. To some extent, the

Table 11. *Agrarian Structure after Land Reform*

Type of Farms	Percentage of		Mean Yield
	Cropland Area	Crop Produced	Quintals/Hectare
Peasant	87	96	13
Group	3	2	10
State	2	2	17

Note: The figures are for major crops, and also do not include farms occupied by, and production of, what are known as permanent crops. Coffee, chat, ensat, fruit farms and the like are excluded.
Source: CSO: *Agricultural Sample Survey, 1979/80, Vol II, Area, Production, Yield, ... of Major Crops*, Addis Ababa, May 1980.

rural economy is in a transitional (or rather fluid) state, and if the government continues to favour the rapid co-operativisation of agriculture, small-holder cultivation may gradually lose its dominance. This is, however, difficult to envisage *at present* because both the process and the level of capital accumulation in the countryside remains unchanged and quite insignificant.

Rural production at present consists of three types of cultivation: small-holder peasant farms, "group cultivation" farms, and large-scale state farms. The second type, that is group cultivation, is made up of joint-cultivation schemes (what are called "Hibret Irshas"), "producers co-operatives", and settlement farms. Both group and state farms are large scale enterprises, use more improved methods and modern inputs, and are given more attention and encouragement by government than peasant farms. However, they make up only a small percentage of rural production. By far the greater portion of the land is under small-holder cultivation which also supplies almost all the agricultural products of the country.

It is interesting to note that in so far as productivity is concerned peasant agriculture appears to be quite competitive. As the table below shows, average yield on state farms is not that much greater than on peasant farms, at least for the one year for which comparative data are available; in this year, yield was 17 quintals per hectare on state farms, and 13 quintals per hectare on peasant farms. The figures are for mean yields of all major crops. In some crops, notably teff, sorghum, millet and all categories of leguminous crops (pulses), average yields on peasant farms are greater than on state farms. This is surprising in wiew of the fact that the latter enjoys high level of investment, uses a great amount of modern inputs, and is highly mechanised, whereas peasant production continues to be as traditional as ever.* The competitiveness of peasant agriculture, however, is not

---

* Recent statements by government officals indicate the performance of state farms has further deteriorated in-absolute terms as well as in relation to individual farms.

Table 12. *Estimate of Area, Production, Yield of Cereals of Peasant Holdings, 1976—1980*

Year	Area In '000 Hect.	Production In '000 Quintals	Yield Quintals/Hectare
1976	4347	44586	10.3
1977	4154	40945	9.9
1978	4383	37417	8.5
1979	4547	38095	8.4
1980*	4150	54917	13.2

Note: The figures are for cereals only, and for the main harvest season.
Source: Ministry of Agriculture: *Area, Production and Yield of Major Crops—in 1974/75—1978/79*. Addis Ababa, July 1979. And CSO (*): ibid.

so much because it has become vigorous and innovative, as because the other forms of cultivation are poorly organised and mis-managed. Whether or not peasant farms will continue to stand up well as against large-scale farms and whether or nor a healthy competition between the forms of agriculture will have a salutary effect on rural production as a whole, is an interresting question, and one worth considering seriously before state policy is irrevocably set in the direction of group cultivation and state farms.

The performance of peasant agriculture since land reform—in all its multiple aspects—is difficult to determine with any degree of accuracy for the reasons mentioned immediately above. The data that appears in the table above covers a period of only five years, that is between the first harvest year of the reform and 1980. It is based on official agricultural surveys conducted throughout the country since 1975; the results of similar surveys after 1980 have not yet been released. The figures must be used with caution, however, because the method of data collection as well as the quality of the data have changed over the years. It is also unfortunate that similar data for pre-reform years are unavailable so that comparative evaluation of the previous land system and the present one with regard to economic performance is precluded.

In view of the reservations noted above regarding the quality of the data, nothing much can be said about the table. If the figures for 1980 are not a result of changes in data collection, and instead indicate a trend, small-holder agriculture may be showing promising signs of improvement. But how far peasant production will continue to develop will depend on the kind of assistance and encouragement it receives from government, and more importantly, on the nature of the relationship it will be able to establish with the urban economy. However, for a reciprocal and mutually invigorating relationship to be set up between town and country, the former must itself, and as a prior condition, go through a metamorphosis, and emerge as the dominant partner in the relation.

Chapter 4

Peasants and Peasant Associations

4.1 Introduction

General

One of the most important aspects of the land reform relates to rural mass organisations which were set up following the first proclamation of 1975. These organisations, of which the local or kebbelle Peasant Association is the most central, were to be in the hands of the peasants themselves, and were to provide the organisational means for administering the land reform, and dealing with social and economic problems arising in the peasant community. The other bodies (which are, however, subordinate to the Peasant Association, and of much less influence) are peasant youth associations, women's associations, and rural defence squads. The Judicial Tribunal—another important institution, but part of the Peasant Association—was also established to enable the peasantry to resolve its own internal conflicts.

It was believed that the peasantry, hitherto unorganised and therefore unable to pursue political goals or to engage in development activities, would be strengthened and activated once it was provided a state-supported apparatus for collective endeavour. The underlying assumption was that the weakness of the peasantry in the past was its lack of organisation, and the Peasant Association, and the other subsidiary bodies, were seen as a remedy for this. These rural organisations, which are open to all peasants, were to enable peasants to give up or modify their isolated and scattered form of existence, and become involved in activities of common concern and benefit.

We have already dealt with the legislation defining the responsibilities and powers of Peasant Associations (PAs) in section 3.1 above. Here, we shall be concerned with how these organisations carry out their duties, how they related to the peasant membership, and what their impact has been on the rural community.

All the proclamations that deal with rural organisations emphasise that the latter are mass organisations whose prime concern is the betterment of the welfare of their members. Membership is not compulsory, but almost all peasants register for membership because it is advantageous to do so. Official sources put the member of primary-level Peasant Associations (PAs) in the country at about 23.5 thousand, involving slightly over 7 million households.[1]

If the figures are accurate, it means that very few peasants remain outside the PA framework, except perhaps those in the pastoral lowlands, and in the marginal areas. The PAs have indeed become an established fact throughout the country, and virtually all peasants come under their authority. This is quite an achievement in itself, for what was a scattered and inaccessible mass of people has now been brought under a network of local organisations.

Tasks of PAs: Rural Development

The major tasks of PAs are economic, and politico-judicial, and may be divided into three broad categories: 1. Land distribution, and land administration; we have already discussed this at length, and we shall not add anything here. 2. Responsibilities associated with rural development. 3. Tasks involving law and order, arbitration, and local administration. We shall discuss the last two, beginning with rural development.

The responsibilities of PAs with regard to rural development are not clearly spelt out in the legislation. There are general provisions that enjoin PAs to strive towards raising production, make improvements in farm methods and technique, and encourage their membership to move towards socialist forms of agriculture. In addition, PAs are required to follow government policy, and to cooperate with concerned agencies in matters related to land use, conservation, and infrastructural projects. Each kebbelle organisation is empowered to establish health, education and marketing services. But how specifically PAs are to encourage development in peasant agriculture, how they are to have access to resources necessary for this effort, and what kind of assistance they are to expect from government, are not fully elucidated.

The formal structure of PAs is logistically well suited to the kind of work involved in rural development and agricultural extension. Each rural kebbelle, i.e., the area over which a PA has jurisdiction, is an agricultural unit with more or less identifiable boundaries, its own resources, a stable population, and an organisational structure. The PA leadership has means—crude though they may be—of communicating with the membership and mobilising them when necessary. Rural development agents, therefore, have much better access to the peasantry now than before. Secondly, the PA is better placed, at least potentially, to acquire for its members modern inputs and other necessary items which would be too costly or inaccessible to individual peasants. Thirdly, the PA, whose power to mobilise peasants is quite remarkable, has the ability, potentially again, to carry out a variety of land improvement and infrastructural projects. By

---

[1] Ministry of Agriculture, *Ke-Yekatit is Yekatit 1973* (Annual Publication of the Ministry), Addis Ababa, 1981.

employing the collective labour of its members alone, it can be involved in drainage and irrigation works, road-building programmes, land reclamation and colonisation schemes, and the like—projects which will benefit all, and have an effect on the performance of rural production. In some areas, rural agents have attempted to use the organisations to set up training and demonstration programmes, and to channel fertilisers and high-yield seeds to the peasantry.

In practice, however, the attempt to involve PAs in development work has proved rather difficult, and the main reasons for this are that PAs do not have (or cannot generate) the resources needed, that they severely lack technical, administrative, and organisational expertise, and that too often they are mostly concerned with preserving what exists rather than changing or developing it. As a result, the method of implementation of rural extension programmes has remained unchanged, and what would have given PAs an important role in servicing their membership is still left to local government agencies.

The problems facing PAs with regard to development work are fundamental. To begin with, the organisations are resourceless, and are in no position to assist peasant agriculture. Their poverty is of course nothing but the poverty of the peasantry at large, but this condition has a serious and debilitating effect on the thinking and attitude of the leadership as well as the membership. It tends to prohibit movement, innovation, planned effort and concern for the collective. It is true that some PAs—mostly woreda PAs—have invested in equipment and land improvement schemes, but these are the exceptions which have been fortunate enough to acquire lucrative assets in the form of cash crop plantations, mills, and small rural workshops. In the majority of cases, however, the condition of PAs is no different from the condition of their membership. Not one of the PAs in the areas of our study had at the time embarked upon self-initiated development schemes of any consequence.

But, it may be argued, if the PAs can mobilise labour—and the Chinese rural experience has shown how important labour mobilisation is–and if this labour is put to good use, this constitutes an effective investment. This is certainly true, however, in many places, PAs have not yet realised what an important resource they have at their disposal. Unless mobilised labour is put to good use, its potential will remain untapped. Although the rural organisations have no difficulty in mobilising peasants, such effort has often been misused. On the other hand, where attempts have, on occasions, been made to utilise peasant labour properly and constructively, the result has been quite impressive. A good example of this comes from Bolloso. With encouragement from outside as well as with their own initiative, peasants here were able to construct 15 rural grade schools serving 7000 peasant pupils, over 200 kms of secondary rural roads connecting those already built by WADU, and dozens of public latrines located at convenient corners throughout the woreda.

The other problem that needs to be raised has to do with the quality of PA leadership. The rural institutions that have been spawned by the land reform are new in concept, and quite different from the traditional forms of rural associations. To be effective and dynamic, they require some expertise, or experience in organisational work, planning and coordination of popular activity. This kind of skill, even of the most rudimentary type, is lacking among a great portion of the officials. The leadership of the PAs is therefore saddled with responsibilities for which its experience and competence is woefully inadequate.

This had led to a situation where many PAs are devoid of initiative, where the resources of their communities are improperly used, and where problems that could easily be overcome by collective effort remain unresolved. We frequently asked PA officials what they believed to be the main tasks of their organisations. The most frequent answers we got were: to implement government directives, and to deal with conflicts that arise in the community. PAs often expect the initiative to come from outside, and they perceive their role to be one of transmitting decisions made elsewhere to their membership.

A third problematic which has a bearing on the potential of PAs for development work is related to the origin of the rural organisations themselves. PAs and their subordinate bodies were established by proclamation by a *new* authority which had just taken political power. The organisations are therefore not only conceptually new, but are also seen as a necessary by-product of the establishment of a new state. Thus the prevalent attitude among many peasants and their leaders is that the PAs are a creation of the state and must therefore be nurtured by the state.

The potential of the organisations as a means of revitalising the rural community, of overcoming the isolation of the population, and of creating a new experience has not been fully realised by peasants and their leadership. In some areas, such as the more inaccessible regions of Sire and Adet, the isolation of the peasants is reflected in the isolation of their Associations, which often have no contact with order PAs, and only have a tenuous link with local government authorities in the woreda. But the PAs are an accepted institution, and have become part of the peasant community.

Tasks of PAs: Administration and Adjudication

The other major tasks of PAs—the political and judiciary—involves responsibility in certain areas of local government, and in adjudication and conflict resolution. It needs to be borne in mind that the land reform has not only changed the agrarian structure of the country but has also done away with the administrative apparatus at the rural or village level.

In the past, a number of officials, some with overlapping authority, were responsible for such essential tasks as law and order, tax collection and the administration of justice in the farming community. In some places, the *chigashum* (or *Qoro* in some southern areas) held in his hand what amounted to full authority for all these tasks. Frequently, however, he was supported by the rural judge, the balabat (where ethnic groups which had a special standing with the state were involved), a sort of vigilante body known as the *Netch-lebash*, and units of a para-military organisation called the Territorial Army if serious security problems arose. The long arm of the state reached the peasant in his rural community through these officials, whose services were also paid for by the peasant himself.

At the woreda level—and this was the unit of state bureaucracy with which the peasant was closely involved—the administrative machinery was a replica in miniature of the awraja and provincial government to which the woreda was subordinate. Administration, adjudication and law enforcement (the police and the prisons) constituted the three elements of local government, each of which was manned by a coterie of junior functionaries who were often incompetent as well as unscrupulous in their dealings with the peasantry. In many cases, and particularly in the southern regions, those who wielded power at all levels, except perhaps the woreda, were "outsiders", that is, men who were not indigenous to the area, and who were unfamiliar with the way of life of the people and insensitive to their needs and problems. Corruption, abuse of power, and embezzlement of state funds by officials at all levels were rampant, and peasants were regularly mistreated as a matter of course.[2]

The administrative restructuring that accompanied the land reform has done away with the old apparatus of authority at the rural or village level. At the woreda level, on the other hand, the machinery of administration has remained by and large intact except that the powers of the law enforcement agencies and the courts have been considerably reduced.

At present, the PA has become tax-collector, policeman and judge within the area of its jurisdiction, the kebbelle, and thereby taken over the tasks of the chiqa-shum, the netch-lebash, and the rural judge all together. It can be said that the PA now forms the lowest adminstrative unit in the structure of provincial and local government inherited and still employed by the new government.

Below the woreda, the essential functions of administration—which still consist of tax-collection, security and law—devolve on the PA, and in consequence, the latter is subordinate to the woreda authority just as the previous offices it had replaced had similarly been. The PA emerges Janus faced, with a dual role and a dual personality: as a mass organisation, it is entrusted with the representation of the interests of the peasantry, and appears as an independent body; as the link in the administrative chain, it is integrated in the machinery of local government and appears as an arm of the state apparatus. This duality has not been without its effect on the performance and leadership of the organisations. Whether to respond to the demands and needs of their membership or those of the administration, whether to represent the peasantry in the state apparatus or

---

[2] For an extended treatment of local government, see J.M. Cohen and P.H. Koehn, *Ethiopian Provincial and Municipal Government* (East Lansing, Michigan State University, African Studies Centre, 1980), chapter III, esp. pp. 27—47. C. Clapham argues that almost all officials at all levels of local government in the south were outsiders; this is exaggerated. "Centralisation and Local Response in Southern Ethiopia", *African Affairs*, vol. 74, no. 294, 197.

the state in the peasantry, whether to give priority to their organisation or administrative duties—such are the hard choices that often face PAs. The choices are made the more difficult because pressure from the local administration is often far greater than that from the peasantry.

That PAs were entrusted with the task of tax-collection is a logical outcome of the land reform. The reform recognises peasants and their organisations as the only force in the rural community, and the old apparatus of control was given no place in the new rural order. The void left by the chiqa-shum and his supporting agents could not be filled by any other body except the PA. The latter was duly empowered to be responsible for tax collection, indirectly at first, and more specifically by the new tax law of 1976. Under this law, it is the duty of each PA to provide a list of all peasants, their holdings and their declared incomes to the tax authorities, and to collect for the latter the land use fee and agricultural income tax from each peasant.[3] The PA will be held accountable if it does not submit what is required of it in time, and also for any tax evasion by peasants in the area.

The task of adjudication and law enforcement has been entrusted to *judicial tribunals* and *rural defence squads* (now called revolutionary defence committees)––both subordinate organs of the PA. The leadership of the latter body was formerly elected from the general assembly and was responsible to it, but recent legislation has changed that, so that now it is a committee elected from among the executive body of the PA and responsible to the executive.

The judicial tribunal, one of the most important bodies in the PA, is a three-man rural court elected by the general assembly of the PA. The powers of the tribunal are much wider than those of the former rural judge that it has replaced. It is competent to hear and pass judgement on the following kinds of disputes: all cases involving land disputes among the membership of the PA; civil and criminal cases in which claims or damages amount up to 500 Birr; and cases involving inheritance and division of property between spouses. In addition, the law provides that any kind of dispute among PA members, or cases where the cause of the dispute has originated within the boundary of the PA can be heard by the tribunal, so long as the parties to the dispute consent to bring them before the tribunal. The judicial tribunals have the power to impose a fine of up to 300 Birr, a prison sentence of up to 3 months, or compulsory labour of up to 15 days.[4]

The judicial tribunal is an important institution in the rural community in that it provides a vehicle for internally resolving conflicts, which otherwise would involve outsiders, that is, the woreda courts and the police. Peasants have easier access to judicial services, and, since tribunal members are peasants themselves and residents of the community, the chances for a timely and sympathetic hearing are better now than before. However, not all peasants consider the tribunals as the ideal solution, and in some areas they have not yet won acceptance from everyone.

---

[3] "Land Use Fee and Agricultural Income Tax Proclamation", op.cit.
[4] For a comparison with the powers of the old rural judge, see Hoben, *Land Tenure* ..., op.cit, p. 79.

In Bolloso and Sire, a great majority of peasants were favourably disposed to their tribunals, in Manna and Adet, on the other hand, quite a number of peasants were dissatisfied with them, and reported that were they given the option they would prefer to take their cases to the regular woreda courts. This is quite surprising in view of the advantages rural courts have over woreda courts, but the main cause of dissatisfaction stems in part from the quality of decisions handed down, and in part from the lack of competence and of professionalism of the tribunal members themselves.

Tribunal members are elected by the general assembly of the PA for a fixed term. This has advantages as well as disadvantages. On the positive side is the fact that those considered best suited to the work will have a better chance of being placed on the "bench"; on the other hand, since office holders are changed periodically, the accumulation of experience and knowledge is sacrificed, and the progressive improvement of the quality of justice made more difficult. Tribunal officers, we found, were often men in their forties and above, although in a few instances younger men in their thirties were also encountered.

Unlike the regular courts, rural tribunals do not have well defined procedures and regular schedules. Meetings are often held irregularly—on rest days, or sometimes at the convenience of officers themselves. Proper records of cases and decisions handed down are not standard practice, but from time to time, when a literate person is available, short reports on what the tribunals have done are prepared and kept at the PA office.

While the kind of corruption and bribe-taking associated with the regular courts were as yet unknown, allegations of unfair practice or nepotism by peasants in our study were not too uncommon. The most serious complaints were, however, that the tribunals were not independent of the PA, and the leadership of the latter—in particular its chairman or executive body—has a strong influence on decisions and settlements. Very often, cases are referred to the tribunals by the executive in which the latter appears, directly or indirectly, as a prosecutor, and tribune members are unwilling to make decisions that are unfavourable to the leadership. Peasants can, of course, appeal to a higher tribunal—that of the woreda—but the appeal process is so time-consuming and inconvenient that many peasants are easily discouraged.

The central leadership of the PA uses the tribunals as a means not only of dealing with inter-peasant conflict but also of extending its own authority. The tribunals are important organs of the PA, and also part of the leadership. Where disputes arise between members and their PAs, tribunals often side with the latter. In short, therefore, judicial tribunals can be a pliable instrument for dictatorial authority in the rural organisations, and unscrupulous leaders—and such leaders have by no means been rare in the PAs—have conveniently used them to serve their own interests.

The judicial tribunals are supported by the rural defence squads (or revolutionary defence committees) established by every PA. The tasks of these law-enforcement bodies include carrying out decisions of the tribunals and the PA leadership, maintaining order, and apprehending law breakers. The active members of the defence squads have been issued arms by the government, and at the time of our field work, all PAs in all woredas had built rural jails which were managed by these armed units. For a time, the defence squads had grown quite powerful vis-a-vis the other leading organs of the PAs, and used to take independent decisions such as putting peasants in detention, confiscating property, etc., without due process or authorisation. In some places, the armed guards were able to subordinate the executive and run the organisations themselves; in others, a collusion between the armed squads and the chairmen of the organisations dominated the PAs. But all this seems to be over now, and the defence squads are firmly under the control of the PA leadership.

The potential of both the judicial tribunals and the defence squads as instruments of rural self-administration are of course quite considerable. But a great deal of enlightenment is necessary both on the part of the leadership as well as the membership for this potential to be realised; peasants must also be fully and actively involved in all aspects of organisational work at the local level—something that is woefully lacking at present. Such involvement can, however, be expected if PAs can play a more effective role in the improvement of peasant life, of agriculture, and in rural development in general.

4.2 Peasant Associations: Structure and Leadership

Structure

Each PA is a "corporate" body with a defined boundary, agricultural resources and its own international administration and leadership. Each peasant household is incorporated in a PA, and its rights of access to land and other resources in the kebbelle are a condition of its membership in the organisation. A peasant household can be a member of only one PA, and it is entitled to land in only one kebbelle. The rural areas are thus partitioned into innumerable "corporate" units each by and large autonomous. A number of these units in a woreda form what is called the woreda PA, an organisation whose task is to coordinate the work of PAs at the kebbelle level; all woreda PAs in an awraja similarly form an awraja PA, and the process is repeated up the ladder to provincial PAs and finally the national body–the *All Ethiopian Peasant Association (AEPA)*.

The leadership of the PA at the kebbelle level consists of what are called "leading organs". Under the most recent PA "Consolidation Proclamation" of 1982, the leading organs are the general assembly of the PA, the executive committee, the inspections committee, and the judicial tribunal. The defence squad (now called the revolutionary defence committee) is under the control of the executive, and is not considered a leading organ.

The general assembly, which is a gathering of all PA members, is the final decision-making body and has the power to set the guidelines of the organisation, and also to elect and remove any and all members of the leading organs. The assembly, however, meets only periodically, and its composition is not always stable.

The subordinate organisations are primarily the peasant youth, and the peasant women's associations, which in turn have their own leading organs and structure of leadership. Both these organisations are appendages of the PA, and are not taken very seriously by the latter or the peasantry at large.

Although in principle the executive committee is responsible for implementing the decisions of the general assembly, and performing the day-to-day activities of the organisation, it is in practice the most powerful organ, and makes all the major decisions. The chairman of the executive—elected and removable by the general assembly—is also the chairman of the PA.

The general assembly is often amorphous and weak, partly because the peasant membership is not quite aware of its own collective power, and partly because the kind of active concern and cohesiveness that makes a deliberative body a dynamic force has yet to appear within the rural community. Its deliberations are easily manipulated by the chairman, or by outsiders such as woreda officials, rural agents, etc. In many instances, it is used either as a sounding board or a rubber stamp, to endorse particular decisions, or to approve measures already taken.

In contrast, the executive is a more cohesive body, consisting at the time of our study, of five elected individuals, and meeting more regularly than the general assembly. The extension of the power of the executive beyond what is prescribed for it by law cannot entirely be blamed on usurpation of power on its part, or the dictatorial intentions of the officers (although such designs are not uncommon). It was also a result of the role the executive plays in PA affairs: it is the officers of the executive who manage the general routine of the organisation, who deal with the problem of individual peasants, and who have access to higher authority in the woreda. To the average peasant, the chairman and his staff *are* the organisation, and he sees his role in the general assembly as no more than supportive or subsidiary.

The inspection committee did not exist at the time of our field work, and was only set up by the 1982 proclamation. Its tasks appear to be that of a watch-dog, an ombudsman, but how it exactly fits in the structure of leadership is not yet clear.

The relationship between one PA and another, or among PAs in a given locality is for the most part superficial. The exception is where neighbouring PAs share resources, such as water, pasture land, woodland, etc., in common. Just as the households in each corporate body are self-provisioning and "atomised", so too, mutual interaction, necessitated by socio-economic interdependence, among the organisations is lacking. The "independence" of the peasant producer, is reproduced in the "independence" of his organisation. This absence of *horizontal integration* among rural organisations is clearly visible in almost all

Chart 1.

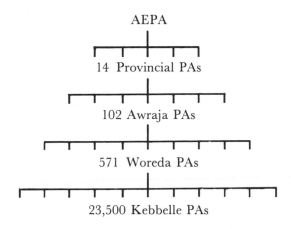

AEPA

14 Provincial PAs

102 Awraja PAs

571 Woreda PAs

23,500 Kebbelle PAs

National Organisational Structure of
Peasant Associations

localities. PAs are, however, *vertically integrated* within a regional and national organisational framework.

The kebbelle PAs in a woreda are subordinate to the woreda PA, which is in turn subordinate to the awraja PA. At the higher level, the provincial PA is responsible for coordinating the work of the awraja PAs, and the national AEPA is at the top of the pyramid. PAs at each level above the kebbelle have their own internal structure, with decision-making vested in what are called congresses and committees, implementation of decisions with executive bodies, and (at the woreda and awraja levels) adjudication in judicial tribunals.

The chart above is a visual representation of the organisational structure of PAs. It will be seen that AEPA at the top of the pyramid is responsible for 14 provincial PAs, 102 awraja PAs, 571 woreda PAs, and 23,500 kebbelle PAs involving about 7 million rural households. This makes the PAs by far the largest organisation in the country.

The woreda PA is the closest to the kebbelles by virtue of its location as well as its accessibility to the leadership of the peasantry. It is therefore easily, and from our experience, frequently involved in kebbelle PA matters. It appears to have the best potential for playing a constructive role in planning and coordinating rural activities at the sub-district level. At present, however, the woreda PAs have very little initiative of their own, and are concerned with two major tasks: to oversee the activities of kebbelle PAs (hardly a worthwhile task), and to transmit government directives downwards. The leadership of the woreda PAs we talked to all emphasised that they considered these to be their most important responsibilities. Supervision took a variety of forms. For one, it involved looking out for kebbelle leaders who were incompetent, untrustworthy or corrupt, and having them replaced by others. This by law is the responsibility of the peasantry itself, but the woreda PAs did not see any contradiction between what they considered to be their supervisory task and the provisions of the law.

In Bolloso and Manna, woreda PA leaders alleged that a large number of kebbelle officials were unwilling to carry out government directives; these they saw as "saboteurs", and unfit to be in positions of leadership. In Sire, woreda leaders were particularly dissatisfied with lower officials who, they said, were reluctant to appear for conferences, and to cooperate in fund-raising activities.

The other form of supervision has to do with resolving disputes within as well as among PAs. Conflicts within a PA may involve factional struggles, conflict over authority, or quarrels arising from improper use of PA property or funds. Disputes between one PA and another in the woreda commonly arise over boundary issues in which a useful asset such as water, woodland, etc. is involved. In either case, woreda PAs are requested to intervene to sort out problems and pacify the warring parties. Their intervention, however, does not always bring about the desired outcome, it may at times exacerbate the conflict.

As one moves up the organisational ladder, the hierarchical bodies not only become further and further removed from the peasantry and the kebbelle leadership, but also increasingly bureaucratic. The primary organisations at the grass-roots level are separated by a wide gulf from those higher above, and a healthy interflow of ideas and initiatives is seriously inhibited. As it is, government directives are channelled downwards, but hardly anything of substance is transmitted upwards from below.

Another problem that must be considered is the nature of the relationship between the primary organisations, i.e. the kebbelle PAs, and the higher-level bodies. These bodies have neither the resources nor the expertise to provide any kind of assistance to peasant agriculture. In some instances, they do not even have enough funds to cover their own running expenses. Moreover, they are not in a position to influence government policy with regard to agricultural prices, credit and related services.

They are thus merely bureaucratic set-ups, and they have no role whatsoever in matters concerning rural development. Peasants and kebbelle PAs turn to the locally based government agencies (such as, for instance, the Ministry of Agriculture) on the woreda administration whenever they need assistance. The PA structure *above* the kebbelle is thus not organically linked with the fundamental needs of the peasantry.

Leadership

Let us now turn to the leadership of the PAs. We shall be concerned with the executive officers of the kebbelle PAs, for these are the most influential leaders in the rural community. By law, PAs should elect officers every two years, but this is not often adhered to in practice. The term of office of a particular leadership may be longer or shorter depending on two important factors: its popularity or unpopularity with officials in the woreda—i.e. the administration or woreda PAs*, or changes in government policy regarding rural organisations. Although the power to elect or remove officials is vested exclusively in the general assembly of PAs, authorities outside the organisation, in particular woreda administration officials and rural development agents, have a great say in who should be elected and who removed. Furthermore, largely at the initiative of such outsiders, officers could be removed before completing their term or retained in office well after their term has expired.

The leaders of the PAs in our study were all men, and we found no women in positions of responsibility—except, of course, in women's associations. This should not come as a surprise, since, as we tried to show earlier, few women are full-fledged members of PAs, and still fewer play an active role in their activities.

It should be noted at the outset—and it will be demonstrated in the course of this discussion—that in sociological terms, the leadership of the rural organisa- tions and their membership are virtually indistinguishable. Distinctions of wealth and status hardly exist between one and the other, and differences in political outlook are likewise not evident. We are here referring to qualitative or substantive differences, and not minor or incidental ones which are to be found even in the most homogeneous of communities. The major effect of the land reform has been universal levelling, in which differences of class and status were eliminated, in which the prevailing socio-economic conditions were more widely spread, and in which the reappearance of social stratification has been made more difficult.

In the following pages we shall present data on three key PA officials, namely chairmen, secretaries and treasurers. We shall first start with a brief personal profile of these officers in the areas of our study.

Elections to office were not often made according to customary practices. In traditional rural associations, older persons are usually chosen to positions of responsibility, for these are considered to be more knowledgeable and more capable. While literacy may have advantages, a person's experience or "wis- dom" (and in the traditional context, this means age), and his standing in the community are given greater value. In the case of PA officials, however, the younger and the more literate are greatly represented in the leadership. It is not quite clear whether this is a result of the recognition on the part of peasants that the new organisations are basically different from the traditional ones and therefore require different personalities and skills, or whether it is the greater influence of outsiders in the election process. It may be a combination of both.

The majority of leaders in all except Adet woreda were young, in their twenties. In Sire, in particular, more than two-thirds of them were in this age

---

* At the time of our field work, what were called rural development or political cadres were not fully active in the peasant community. Also, COPWE had not been established at the awraja or woreda level.

Table 13. *Previous Status of Selected PA Leaders*

Woreda	Land-lord	Owner-cultivator	Tenant	Wage labour	Mixed owner	Land-less	Others*	Total
Bolloso	—	12(67)	3(17)	—	—	—	3(17)	18(101)
Manna	—	5(26)	6(32)	1(5)	1(5)	2(11)	4(21)	19(100)
Adet	1(3)	14(48)	3(10)	—	10(35)	—	1(3)	29(99)
Sire	—	1(4)	13(48)	—	—	2(7)	11(41)	27(100)

Note: Figures in brackets are %.
* This column includes those who were minors before reform.

group. That literacy was considered an asset in office holders is confirmed by the fact that there were proportionally more literate persons in the leadership than in the general membership in each area. In Adet about half of the office holders were literate, and, in Sire, more than two-thirds of them had some formal education.

It has been argued by some that the leadership of the rural organisations are dominated by those who were previously in privileged positions, that is former landlords, or well-to-do peasants, and that the majority of peasants who were tenants or poor have been excluded from office.[1] Others further add that the PA leadership can be considered a distinct group of middle or rich peasants which has benefitted the most from the land reform at the expence of the great mass of the peasantry.

Table 13 gives a breakdown of the status of peasants in the leadership before the land reform. We see here that the leadership is composed of a cross-section of the peasantry, and that it has not been captured by any distinct group, much less by those who were formerly the more prosperous elements. The majority of leaders are drawn from former owner-cultivators and tenants and in each area, the particular composition is no different from that of the membership, as a comparison with a similar table in section 3.4 above reveals.

To take just one illustration: a majority of the peasants in Bolloso (about 62%) were previously owner-cultivators, and about the same percentage are represented in the leadership (67%) as shown in the table. With the exception of Adet, former landlords do not appear in the leadership at all, and the strength of these in Adet is not very significant. It is worth noting that a small percentage of peasants in Manna and Sire who formerly were landless dependents are among the leadership. This is not to deny that in the coming years the PAs may be

---

[1] A Soviet commentator suggests as much. See G. Galperin, "Ethiopia: Stages of Agrarian Revolution", *Asia and Africa Today* (Moscow), No. 6, 1981. This same author also alleges that kulaks are sabotaging the land reform, an argument which is completely unfounded.

Table 14. *Distribution of Oxen among PA Leaders (%)*

Woreda	% of Leaders Owning						
	0	½*	1	2	3	4	5+
Bolloso	17	5	72	5	—	—	—
Manna	35	5	35	25	—	—	—
Adet	3	—	41	55	—	—	—
Sire	7	—	22	70	—	—	—

*½ means one animal owned in common by two individuals. Compare with Table 6 above.

dominated by stronger peasants, but the evidence we have shown does not support the view that this is the case at present.

This, by itself, however, does not prove whether or not the leadership *now* is different in social terms from its membership, whether or not it has sufficient economic power to be considered a distinct social group. In order to establish that we need to make a comparison between the "wealth" of the leadership and that of the membership. The Ethiopian peasant's capital consists of land, means of cultivation and livestock. Let us look at the distribution of means of cultivation and land among the leadership.

Table 14 reveals that a far smaller percentage of officials are *short* of farm oxen as compared to ordinary peasants in their respective areas, and a larger percentage own 1 or 2 oxen. This is significant, because, as is very well known, oxen determine the level of income as well as the degree of material dependence of rural cultivators. But a close examination of the figures indicates that the leadership are no more a privileged social group than ordinary peasants with oxen are.

As far as the holdings of PA officials are concerned, our findings reveal that both leaders and led equally belong to the same class of petty producers. As the figures in Table 15 show, the pattern of holdings of officials in each region corresponds very closely with that of peasant holdings locally.

In Bolloso woreda, for instance, none of the officials in our sample held land over 1 hectare in size; a great majority of them were mini-holders of half a hectare or less. In Adet, on the other hand, mini-holders are a small percentage, and about one-third of the leadership holds land between 3 and 5 hectares. In both cases, however, the distribution is not too different from that of their respective PA memberships.

Office holding does not involve any special privileges, at least not in principle. Those who have been elected as leaders of PAs are neither paid salaries nor given any material advantages. This, coupled with the fact that officers are often not secure in their positions, that they are quickly and unexpectedly replaced, has so far militated against the capture of the organisations by particular interest groups. In a way this may be positive, but it is also a reflection of the weakness

Table 15. *Distribution of Holdings of PA Leaders. Pre- and Post Reform* (%)

		To 0.25	0.26 -0.50	0.51 -0.99	1.00 -1.25	1.26 -1.50	1.51 -1.99	2.00 -2.50	2.51 -2.99	3.00 -3.99	4.00 -4.99	5.00 -5.99	6 and over
Bolloso	Pre-	47	33	20	—	—	—	—	—	—	—	—	—
	Post-	28	61	11	—	—	—	—	—	—	—	—	—
Manna	Pre-	42	8	8	8	8	—	—	—	—	8	17	—
	Post-	5	21	47	16	—	—	5	5	—	—	—	—
Adet	Pre-	4	—	—	4	—	11	21	4	21	14	—	7
	Post-	—	—	3	17	—	7	35	7	24	7	—	—
Sire	Pre-	—	9	55	27	9	—	—	—	—	—	—	—
	Post-	4	7	63	11	11	4	—	—	—	—	—	—

Note: Not all peasants with 6 hectares and over were landlords. Size in hectares.

and instability of the Associations which have not evolved into an independent and self-assertive rural force. The transfer of leadership in an orderly way has not been institutionalised, and frequent changes, induced for the most part by outside forces, is significantly high. As a consequence, the PAs have not been able to develop a stable leadership, and however respected and popular a leadership may be among the peasant membership, it lacks the kind of strong backing from the members to enable it to stand on its own feet and resist pressures from outside.

The number of PA officials who had been prematurely relieved of their posts was quite considerable. In Manna, for example, the chairmen of 5 PAs were replaced more than 6 times up to the time of our field work. The reasons for this high rate of turnover were numerous, but the most frequently cited were corruption and improper use of authority. Officials at the woreda administration alleged that corruption among peasant leaders was rampant, and that without close supervision from their office the rural organisations would degenerate into the personal fiefdoms of the unscrupulous, or become sources of lucrative gain for a few individuals. PA officials at the woreda level were also forthright in their criticism of corruption among kebbelle officials, although corruption was one among a number of short-comings cited—incompetence, uncooperative attitudes, refusal to carry out directives from above, being the others.

Woreda officials as a whole tend to exaggerate the level of corruption among PAs, partly to justify their own frequent interference in the activities of the latter, and partly to appear in the eyes of higher authorities as the champions of peasant interests and welfare. Some of the accusations of malpractice were either unfounded or difficult to prove. It is, however, undeniable that a number of peasant leaders were not free from corruption, and that a considerable degree of abuse of authority was not uncommon. Our own assessment, based on interviews with peasants and peasant leaders, is that corruption was widespread enough to be of serious concern to the health of the organisations, but that its magnitude had been exaggerated. Given the fact that the peasantry is inexperienced in organisational matters, a certain degree of corruption by its leadership should not come as a surprise. But this has often been magnified to serve as an excuse for interfering in the "internal affairs" of the peasantry, and undermining the authority of the PAs' decision-making bodies.

The most common kinds of corruption were embezzlement, mis-use of PA property, and fraud. In addition, some peasants complained that PA officials were often guilty of nepotism.

The general assembly of the PA is frequently not the prime mover in cases involving dismissal of corrupt officials, and in point of fact, it plays a minimal role in the proceedings. The method of removal of officials accused of corruption is not uniform but depends on the discretion of the accusers themselves. If the accusers are outsiders, i.e. woreda officials, it is done in one of the following ways. In some places, a meeting of the leadership is called, and those alleged to be corrupt are dismissed right there and then. In others, dismissal takes place at a gathering of the PA membership, and new ones are elected on the spot. At times those accused of having perpetrated misdeeds alone are relieved of their posts, at others, the alleged perpetrators along with the rest of the leadership are thrown out. On occasions, accused officials are put in detention on the order of woreda officials.

The relation between the kebbelle leadership and the woreda PA officials was one in which neither of the parties was satisfied with the work of the other, and in which there was a great deal of distrust on both sides. Kebbelle leaders often complained that the woreda PA was not responsive to their needs, that it was by and large an extension of the woreda administration, and that whenever its officers came to the kebbelles it was merely to order people about or to collect funds. Some woreda PAs were considered to be highly authoritarian, and in Manna woreda, the leadership at the time of our fieldwork was said to have been personally handpicked by the incumbent woreda administrator. Allegations of corruption by some kebbelle officials against their counterparts in the woreda were not uncommon. Indeed, some of the woreda PA leaders we talked to were expensively dressed for peasants, and affected the worst mannerisms of civil service bureaucrats.

PAs and Local Government

A brief account of the relations of Peasant Associations with the woreda administration—the lowest unit of local government in Ethiopia—will now be given.

We may begin by noting that the woreda administration is responsible for everything that takes place in the woreda. While other government agencies, such as, for example, the Ministry of Agriculture, of Finance, etc., are also involved in the woreda, their work is a specialised one, whereas the administration is a sort of supra-agency that oversees other agencies, and has a say in what is done, or what is not done, in the area. The supervision of tax-collection, law and order and security have traditionally been under its authority and still are today; but in addition, it is involved in all aspects of rural organisational work.

Within the structure of provincial and local government, the power and functions of the woreda administration have by and large remained unchanged, and at present, and as a result of land reform, it has become closely involved in virtually all phases of the work of rural organisations. Legally, the PAs are not subject to the authority of the administration insofar as their internal affairs are concerned, but the law makes them responsible for following and implementing government policies and directives; this provides the administration, as an agent of government and through which many of the policies or directives are channelled down, some basis for being concerned about PA activities. The law, however, is one thing, what happens in practice is quite another. In practice, the administration oversees PA elections, determines who in the leadership should be removed and who should replace him, initiates the auditing of PA records, investigates real or alleged cases of mismanagement, and acts as an arbitrator when disputes among PAs arise. From time to time, the office organises seminars or conferences for peasant leaders to acquaint them with new government policies and directives. Meetings are also called to raise funds for a variety of purposes.

It is true on occasions the woreda delegates other government agencies to carry on some of these tasks, but in continues to keep in close touch even when it is not directly involved.

The administration plays a key role in the continuing formation and re-formation of rural organisations. Although PAs have been established in all parts of the country, and have been operating for several years, a good deal of re-structuring and re-arrangement is still going on. For convenience or better management, for reasons having to do with major rural development projects, or by a decision of higher authorities, PA boundaries (or, at times woreda boundaries as well) are re-drawn. The result often is that PAs have to be established afresh, or existing ones substantially re-structured. A few months before we started field work in Adet, the entire rural organisations in the woreda were re-organised, and by a series of mergers the number of PAs reduced almost by half. This restructuring process also involves PA service cooperatives, peasant youth and women's associations, and other subordinate bodies. The woreda administration coordinates and supervises the whole process.

The woreda administration also initiates or is actively involved in plans for community work programmes—such as the building of multi-purpose agricultural centres, public squares or sports fields, etc.—which may involve a large number of peasants and PAs. In addition to this, there are community activities which are political in nature. Mass rallies during political holidays, political education conferences, and public festivities of one sort or another are quite frequent in the rural areas. The woreda office is the major organiser here too. Finally, from time to time, the leadership of all the PAs in the woreda meet together either to elect officers to the woreda PA, or delegates to represent the woreda at some occasion elsewhere. Here again, the administrator, together with officers from the other local agencies, plays a central role, often considerably influencing the outcome of the proceedings.

It may be thought that a great deal of what the administration does in connection with rural organisations is the responsibility of the woreda PA, and it should be this office which should be the chief organiser of peasants and relevant work programmes.

This is valid in principle, but in practice the woreda PA is greatly over-shadowed by the administration and the local government agencies by its lack of initiative and organisational know-how. The woreda PA does not have the same kind of authority among peasants and PAs as the administration. The authority of the latter is recognised by the PAs, and this explains in part the preponderant influence of the administration in their own affairs.

Local government does not, however, speak with one voice or act with unanimity. What PAs are told by one government official is contradicted or reversed by another, which often throws PAs into confusion. This is the more so because woreda administrators and rural agents do not often stay in one place for long, and there is a constant reshuffling of personnel at the local level. During our field work which lasted about six months, two of the woreda administrators started work about the same time we did, and two of the others, who had been on the job for about a year, were transferred elsewhere shortly after. The turn-over among rural agents is also quite high, and frequently agents are removed before they have had time to complete programmes they had started.

4.3 Peasants and Peasants Associations

Peasant Participation

The participation of the rural population in organisational activity has been highly uneven, and the PAs have gradually lost the popular enthusiasm they had at the initial period of the land reform. At the time of their formation, and during land distribution, peasants had shown a good deal of active concern for their organisations, even though there was a certain measure of uncertainty about the reform and a considerable degree of confusion in the rural areas due to the opposition of landlords and their associates. At present, peasant attitude to the PAs is ambivalent, and PA attempts to mobilise effort for community work are not enthusiastically received.

It is not that peasants reject the organisations in principle, on the contrary, a great majority of them consider the PAs as a part of land reform. The problem is tied to a large variety of factors: the quality of leadership, the purpose of general assembly gatherings, the fact that a great many demands are put on peasants by PAs, the fact that PAs have not enabled peasants to improve the quality of their lives, etc.

The frequency of gatherings of the general assembly varies considerably among PAs and regions. In Bolloso woreda, for instance, some PAs said they held meetings every fortnight, others every month. In the majority of cases, meetings are held irregularly, whenever the need arises, or whenever higher authorities demand them. It is not very easy to gather together the general membership, especially in areas where peasants live in dispersed settlements such as Adet or Sire. Information about meetings is passed on by word of mouth, and in scattered settlements it might take several days before all members are informed. Meetings are called not only to discuss PA matters, but to instruct members to take part in community work programmes, to participate in political rallies, or to receive dignitaries that may be visiting the area. Quite often, the purposes for which meetings are called are not related directly to the concrete problems of the community.

Attendance at general assembly meetings has become a problem which is worrying a good number of PA leaders who admit that the gatherings are not as well attended as they would wish. Many peasants do not choose to talk about the assemblies or their participation in them openly and frankly, but those who do, complain that the meetings have become forums for endless wrangling on petty issues, or convenient platforms for launching fund-raising campaigns. When we asked peasants and their leaders whether or not members attended meetings voluntarily, we obtained two different answers. A large number of peasants themselves answered that their participation in meetings was voluntary, but many PA officials reported that members attend meetings because they are afraid of being penalised if they do not.

Almost all PAs have instituted various forms of penalties against those who fail to show up at meetings. The most common ones are cash fines, compulsory labour, detention, or a combination of labour and detention. Fines vary from 0.25 cents for each day of absence (Adet) to up to 2 Birr (Sire). Very often, however, compulsory labour is the most common form of punishment, and in the more serious cases, that is for those who either boycott meetings altogether, or do not show up for important ones, labour is combined with detention. PA leaders are not really happy with this form of imposing discipline among their member-ship but, they argue, there is no other way of inducing peasants to be more concerned about the activities of their organisations. The number of peasants actually penalised for not attending meetings was, however, not very high; officials were reluctant to hand out penalties for they feared that in the end that would be counter-productive.

General assemblies are not only poorly attended, but the manner in which discussions are conducted and decisions adopted leaves much to be desired. It is of course unrealistic to expect PAs to run meetings·properly and with professio-nal competence, but what takes place in gatherings at times falls far short of what is acceptable under the circumstances. Quite often, the discussions are one-sided, with the leadership doing all the talking, and peasants on the whole passive and quiet. On occasions when officials from the woreda are present, the assemblies are turned into lecture forums, with the officials giving long speeches which are often laced with the latest political jargon. The practice of delivering long sermons which are invariably dull and irrelevant, and full of meaningless slogans, has become frequent even among the leadership of the PAs. At the end of the speech-making, the assembly is instructed to endorse plans or decisions presented to it by the organisers.

Relations between Peasants and PAs

Peasant attitude to the PAs is a mixture of appreciation and toleration, supporti-veness and resentment, depending on the leadership and the actions they take or fail to take. The leaders of rural organisations are familiar faces, they speak the same language, live in the same locality, and are often just as poor as everybody else. Unlike the authorities from outside, who are both distant as well as different, peasant leaders are more accessible. This is the positive side of the organisations. However, the PAs are not independent of outside forces: they frequently carry out measures that are unpopular, and put a great deal of demands on peasants. This tends to distance them from the general membership. This dual character of PAs—of being at once close and distant, part of the community and at the same time part of the outside world–is responsible for the kind of ambivalent attitude of peasants to the organisations.

Peasants are not unaware that there is corruption among their officials, but the average peasant is not very much perturbed by such practices as misappropriation of PA funds or property. Both in rural and urban Ethiopia, the office holder who lines his pocket—discretely and moderately, of course—does not suffer from public opprobrium, it being generally accepted that this is one of the benefits of holding a post. What peasants find most unacceptable is when officials use their authority to mistreat individuals, either as a means of settling personal accounts, or of depriving them of their property. Incidents of this sort have been quite frequent in the rural areas, and a few of the sensational ones were even reported in the national press. Individual peasants were physically abused, improperly and unjustly put in detention, or dispossessed of their property illegally by unscrupulous PA officials in a number of peasant communities.

Relations between peasants and peasant leaders, and among the membership as well, are not always free of conflict and tension. Conflicts also exist within the leadership itself. Not all the causes of disputes and quarrels are easy to fathom, since some of them had their origin in the distant past, and under circumstances which are now too obscure or too intricate to be grasped by outsiders. The most common sources of friction that we were able to identify were the following: 1. conflicts within the leadership based on factional struggles for power and influence; 2. conflicts within the leadership and the membership based on ethnic, clan and/or religious differences; 3. conflicts between the leadership and the younger members of the peasantry; 4. conflicts based on personal differences. The latter is such a common feature of both rural and urban organisations in Ethiopia that we shall leave it out of the discussion.

The factional struggles which sometimes occurred in rural organisations were centred around groupings vying for power in the PAs. The conflict may have had its origin within the leadership or the community at large (often the former), or it may have been an extension of the rivalry and conflict among authorities from outside. This kind of struggle was not too common to begin with, and is becoming more and more infrequent now. One example will serve as an illustration. At the time of our field work, some of the leadership of a number of PAs in Manna were supporters of the incumbent woreda administrator, and a few others of the administrator previous to him. In both cases, it appears some impropriety involving PA property had taken place and both factions were in one way or another implicated. Each side was attempting to dislodge the other from the leadership and to make it accountable for all that had happened. In the process, the organisations became battlegrounds in which some of the *membership* were drawn into the conflict on one side or the other. During land distribution, some peasants were rewarded and others penalised depending which side they had supported. By the time our field work was completed and we were about to leave, the woreda administrator was transferred elsewhere, and there was an uneasy truce among the warring factions.

The most serious source of conflict is where there are ethnic, clan or religious differences in the community. In a large number of cases, the kebbelle PA, restricted as it is to a small geographical area, is composed of a homogeneous community, both culturally and ethnically. This is the case, for instance, in Adet and Sire. Furthermore–and this is an important point–the land reform, particularly in the southern regions (in areas predominantly Oromo, or of minority nationalities), has eliminated landlord settlers of northern origin, which previously were a dominant force, and a cause of ethnic/tribal conflict. However, in some areas, the kebbelle communities are not entirely homogeneous, and consist of elements from different religious, ethnic and/or clan backgrounds. At times, a culturally homogeneous community–i.e. a community made up of a single nationality–may be differentiated along religious lines. This is the case, for instance, in Bolloso, where the peasantry is entirely of Wollaita origin, but where a small and active minority made up of non-Coptic Christian converts exists.

The conflicts that arise in these conditions are at times quite sharp, and threaten to split the organisations apart. Usually, hostilities which had been latent all along erupt in the open when the contest for leadership involves individuals from different faiths or cultural backgrounds. In Bolloso, the converts were quite active in some PAs, and the conflicts that arose among the peasantry here were serious enough to take up a great deal of the time of the woreda adminstrator and the woreda PA office.

The conflict between the old and the young was not so much a result of a generational gap or of differences in outlook, as a conflict tied up with the land reform itself.

Young members of PAs, who have joined the PAs recently, especially after land distribution had been completed, often end up with the poorest and the smallest land allotments. This is not, in fairness to the leadership, a result of deliberate discrimination against the young, but of the fact that the available land has already been allocated to peasants, and there is just no excess land to distribute. The young peasants, however, feel unfairly treated and resentful of the leadership. It is these kinds of peasants who often are quite forthright in their criticism of the failings of PA officers, and even the PA itself.

Yet, these conflicts, serious though some of them may be, do not pose a serious threat to the rural organisations. What peasants are seriously apprehensive about is the growing power of the leadership, particularly the executive, which has become the sole authority for allocating rural resources. The power of the executive has become inflated because among other things it has the discretionary power to redraw allotment boundaries and by this means to reward or penalise peasants. In theory, the peasants, through the general assembly, can curb the power of the executive, or even replace the entire leadership, but in practice, the chairman and the executive exercise a dominant influence in the organisation.

Conclusion

The PAs are the basic channel of communication between the state and the peasantry. They have become the main link between the outside world and the rural world and any activity in the rural areas—be it extension or development work, literacy or public health programmes, data collection or plain tourism—is carried out through them. They are instrumental in mobilising the population when necessary, in obtaining the cooperation of the peasantry without which no rural programmes can be successful, in transmitting information or guidelines, etc.

The peasantry as a whole has been incorporated into a *vast network* of geographically defined and distinct "corporate" bodies. Each peasant now has a specific location in the network, a specific, legally recognised corporation with which he is intimately associated by economic necessity and ties of membership. What this means is that the peasant is far more *accessible to the outside world* now than ever before, although, insofar as the relation of the peasant to the world outside, and his access to it is concerned, the situation remains unchanged.

Chapter 5

Peasants and Agrarian Reform

A Summary of the Issues

As the experience of a number of countries has shown, agrarian reform, both in theory and practice, raises just as many problems as it solves.

In the Marxist classics, the agrarian question has been given very little treatment. Marx and Engels were concerned mostly with the development of industrial capitalism, and with the struggle of the urban proletariat which was unfolding at the time. The rural producer, in particular the small-holding peasant, was a problem that did not quite fit into the general scheme of socialist theory, and they both looked at the peasant mode of production as a historical relic destined to disappear. Both writers were convinced that in the long run, that once capital invades the countryside, the peasant and his antediluvian world would be eliminated and replaced by the rural proletariat whose relations to capital and whose political interests would be identical to those of the industrial proletariat.[1]

To Marx, the agrarian problem was associated with capitalism, a problem whose solution lay in the socialisation of agricultural production. The question as it appears in pre-capitalist or proto-capitalist societies such as we have in many parts of the Third World today—that is, the question of peasant dependency and landlordism, of land reform and distribution of rural assets, etc.—hardly concerned Marx for the reason that in the areas of Europe that attracted his attention most, this particular form of the problem had been dealt with by the capitalist revolution. In the one case, i.e. in pre-capitalist conditions, the problem calls for reforms that are distributive in nature, in the other, reforms that are collectivist or associative.

We must thus note that the content of the problem no less than its solution is different in different contexts, and that, for example, collectivisation of agriculture is not a universal remedy. Where Marx posed the socialisation of rural production as a solution, he did so under specific circumstances and in the framework of definite social relations. In fact, what is a solution under one set of circumstances can become a problem under another.

In a note drafted as a response to Bakunin, Marx suggests what reform must or

---

[1] A review of Marx's arguments about peasants appears in my *Marx and Peasant Societies*, Institute of Development Research Occasional Paper No. 15, Addis Ababa University, 1981.

must not consist of insofar as small-holding peasants are concerned. Where, in the exceptional circumstance, the proletariat has assumed power in a predominantly peasant society, it must take

> governmental measures directly to improve the peasant's conditions, so as to win him over to the revolution; measures however, that in their seed facilitate the transition from private land ownership to collective ownership, so that the peasant arrives at it economically himself; but the government must not offend the peasant by proclaiming, for example, the abolition of the right of inheritance, or the abolition of his property; the latter is possible only where the capitalist tenant has displaced the peasant, and the real farm worker is as much a proletarian, a wage-labourer, as the city worker ... . Still less must parcelled property by strengthened by increasing the size of the parcels through the simple annexation of the large estates by the peasants ... .[2]

For the small peasants, the remedy is not the abolition of individual property, on the contrary, reform must consist of the following measures:

1. to improve directly the general condition of peasants. It appears that such improvement must come about through economic and fiscal assistance to peasants, for arguments are raised against the enlargement of peasant holdings by annexation of the large estates;

2. the state should not antagonise the peasant by abolishing the right of inheritance or private property;

3. the peasant's eventual transition from private to collective ownership should be facilitated; the decision to give up his private plots is to be made by the peasant himself, because of his own recognition that it is economically beneficial to do so.

Collectivisation is a goal, but it will be possible when rural production has become capitalistic, and when the real producer is a rural proletarian and not a peasant.

The argument of Engels with respect to collectivisation is in the main similar to that of Marx. He too insists that large-scale and capitalist enterprises should be converted into socialist enterprises. Indeed, the transformation of capitalistically operated large-scale farms "into socialist enterprises is here fully prepared for and can be carried into execution overnight."[3] Engels cautions, however, that the socialisation of agriculture is not a universal solution, and that it should be undertaken primarily in those countries "where there is large land ownership, with large agricultural enterprises, with one master and many wage-workers in

---

[2] "Conspectus on Bakunin's *State and Anarchy*" in Saul K. Padover (ed.), *The Karl Marx Library, vol. 3, on the First International* (New York: McGraw-Hill, 1973), p. XXXVII. For his argument against socialisation of agriculture under conditions of small-holding production, see his "The Nationalisation of the Land," in Marx and Engels, *Selected Works in Three Volumes,* vol. 2, (Moscow: Progress Publishers, 1969).

[3] "The Peasant Question in France and Germany" (1894), in Marx and Engels, *Selected Works in Two Volumes,* vol. 2 (Moscow: Progress Publishers, 1962), p. 438.

every estate."[4] But insofar as the small-holding peasant is concerned, the problem is far from straightforward.

Engels is convinced that the peasant is "irretrievably doomed;" he is threatened from all sides—by the continuously expansive capitalist estates with whom we cannot compete, by the stagnant and indeed regressive nature of his own production, and by debts and mortgages which progressively ruin his economy.

Such being his fate, the remedy lies not in maintaining his petty production, but rather in moving towards large-scale and cooperative production. However, Engels understands that the peasant's resistance to giving up his property is strong and a programme of this sort will not be accepted. Initially, therefore, attempts must be made to improve the conditions of the peasant by measures of a fiscal nature, i.e. financial assistance, the reduction of his debts and obligations, and the eliminations of his dependence on usurers and outside forces.[5] Gradually, by "dint of example" the peasant is to be led towards cooperative forms of production, i.e. production in which the land belongs to the producers themselves, and work is carried on in common. Engels is aware that this process, i.e. the transition to cooperative forms of production, is a long-term one and the proletarian state can do nothing to hasten it against the will of the peasant except to offer assistance and encouragement.

While Marx and Engels dealt with the agrarian problem in the abstract, in anticipation of a proletarian revolution, Lenin was confronted with it concretely at the time of the Bolshevik revolution. On the morrow of the Bolshevik seizure of power, Lenin proclaimed the "Decree on Land" which called for the nationalisation of land, and which put the land of the nation at the disposal of peasants organised in their local Peasant Soviets. In effect, this decree provided for the distribution of land to peasants, and the question of the socialisation of agriculture was not given any serious consideration.[6] Indeed, Lenin strongly argued that agrarian reform is not a socialist programme, but rather a bourgeois-democratic one, and that it should therefore entail "freedom of land tenure from all non-bourgeois adjuncts to the greatest possible degree conceivable in a capitalist society."[7] He scoffed at his pro-peasant opponents, the Socialists, who called for the socialisation of agriculture on the grounds that the Russian peasant had acquired a measure of socialist consciousness through his experience in the traditional rural commune. He was acutely aware that to preserve the support of the peasant for the new state, the peasant's land hunger must be satisfied, and his security in his holding strengthened. A pro-

---

[4] *The Peasant War in Germany*, 1870 edn. (New York: International Publishers, 1966), p. 20.

[5] Ibid, p. 19.

[6] See "The Decree on Land" in Lenin, *Selected Works in Three Volumes,* vol. 2 (New York: International Publishers, 1967), pp. 467–70.

[7] "Resolution on the Agrarian Question," ibid, p. 101. For a brief discussion of the agrarian reform measures of the Bolsheviks in 1917–18, see A. Hussain and K. Tribe, *Marxism and the Agrarian Question,* vol. 2, *Russian Marxism and the Peasantry 1861–1930* (London: Macmillan Press, 1981), esp. pp. 95–101.

gramme of agrarian socialism, which would involve in effect the expropriation of the peasant would be counter-productive.

A few years later, he argued that for collective forms of agriculture to be possible the preconditions for them must first be laid down, namely that the proletarian state must *in advance* re-organise *industry* and develop it "on the lines of large-scale collective production and on a modern technical basis." This alone will

> enable the cities to render such radical assistance, technical and social, to the backward and scattered rural population as will create the material basis necessary to boost the productivity of agriculture and of farm labour in general, thereby encouraging the small farmers by the force of example and in their own interests to adopt large-scale, collective and mechanised agriculture.[8]

Thus the structural weakness of peasant production—a weakness which was not only technological but also social—its inability to transcend its own limitations was to be *overcome from outside,* by advanced socialist industrialisation. In the meantime, that is, until the cities came to the assistance of the countryside, private enterprise (albeit its petty-commodity production variant) was to co-exist side by side with socialist industrial enterprise. The concrete reality of the rural world *even* after land reform, namely, extreme backwardness of technique, scattered and subsistence production, medieval forms of culture and social relations, could not be conjured away by blind faith or revolutionary slogan-eering. Here we have Lenin the pragmatist: what is objectively possible must take precedence over what is ideologically necessary.

A short while before he died, Lenin saw in co-operatives *the* solution not only to the agrarian problem but also to that of the transition to socialism as a whole. So strongly convinced was he about this that he virtually equated socialism with the development of co-operatives, although he recognised at the same time that the latter task presented immense difficulties.

> If the whole of the peasantry had been organised in cooperatives, we would by now have been standing with both feet on the soil of socialism. But the organisation of the entire peasantry in co-operative societies presupposes a standard of culture among the peasants ... that cannot, in fact, be achieved without a cultural revolution ... . This cultural revolution would now suffice to make our country a completely socialist country ... .[9]

It is important to note that the co-operatives Lenin had in mind were *not* production co-operatives but rather marketing and trading ones. We must also observe that in this particular essay, collectivisation, socialisation of agriculture proper, has been relegated to some time in the distant future, to a period beyond socialism.

---

[8] "Preliminary Draft Theses on the Agrarian Question," in ibid., vol. 3, p. 436.
[9] 'On Co-operation', in ibid., p. 764.

In summary, the common thread that runs through Marx, Engels and Lenin is that agrarian reform must be an all-round measure that will unleash a host of economic, social and technical forces which will *subvert* the rural economy, undermine its resilence, and promote the progressive dissolution of the peasant mode of production. On the other hand, the Marxist classics caution us against precipitate collectivisation in conditions in which the prerequisites for doing so are not already given, where, that is, the productive forces in their technical and social forms are severely underdeveloped.

Now, it is our contention that the forces that will transform the peasant mode of production are to be found not in the countryside but outside it, and rural development is at bottom nothing other than "urban" development transposed to the countryside. By eliminating landlordism and peasant dependency, agrarian reform offers the peasant only his autonomy, but the autonomy of the rural producer will become a productive force if it is converted, in the sphere of material production, into a new form of 'dependency' in which the city, considered here as the generative power in society, not only assumes the previous role of the landlord with regard to surplus extraction but provides the impulse and the rationale for peasant production: Social freedom accompanied by economic incorporation leading to the re-integration of the country into the city, or as Marx would say, the urbanisation of the countryside.

The obverse of this is that reform will strengthen the peasant's primordial selfish instincts, and transform peasant autonomy into a limitation by making the rural world a world in itself. Having appeased the peasant's hunger for land or removed the landlord's stranglehold over him,ʼ reform may in the process promote the further peasantisation of rural society, whereby the peasant world turns inward rather than outward, widens the gulf between it and the rest of society, and denies the emergence of new productive energy and new social actors. This danger is the more likely in rural economies such as Ethiopia's, where, for the most part, peasant production is not dependent on or integrated into a national economic framework, but is characterised by independence and segmentation. Here one region has virtually no intercourse with another, and famine in one district and a bumper harvest next door are not uncommon occurrences. Moreover, the city cannot come to the active assistance of the country for the reason that the former is subordinate to the latter. The major concern of agrarian policy, therefore, must be to reverse this relationship in a radical way.

Select Bibliography

Abbreviations

AMC=Agricultural Marketing Corporation. CSO=Central Statistical Office. CADU=Chillalo Agricultural Development Unit. IDR=Institute of Development Research (Addis Ababa University). PMAC=Provisional Military Administrative Council. WADU=Wollaita Agricultural Development Unit.

Official Publications

Publications by the various Government agencies are published by the authorities concerned.

AMC: 'Report on Grain Purchasing and Distribution' (in Amharic). Unpublished mimeo, Addis Ababa, 1981.

CSO: *Agricultural Sample Survey 1979/80*. Vol. II, *Area, Production, Yield,... of Major Crops*. Addis Ababa, May 1980. Vol. III, *Farm Buildings and Implements*, July 1980. Vol. IV, *Cost of Production of Major Crops*, July 1980.

—:*Analysis of Demographic Data*. Statistical Bulletin No. 16, Addis Ababa, December 1974.

—:*Results of the National Sample Survey, 2nd Round*, vol. V., *Land Area and Utilisation*, Addis Ababa, February 1975.

Faculty of Law: *Consolidated Laws of Ethiopia*, Vol. I Addis Ababa: Haile Selassie University, 1972.

Ministry of Agriculture: *Agricultural Sample Survey 1974/75*, vols. I and II. Addis Ababa, July and September 1975.

—:*Area, Production, and Yield of Major Crops ... 1974/75–1978/79*, Addis Ababa, July 1979.

—:*Ke-Yekatit isk Yekatit* (Annual Amharic Publication), Addis Ababa, 1981 issue (1973 Eth.'n Cal.).

—:*Report of the Crop Condition Survey*. Addis Ababa, 1974.

Ministry of Land Reform: *Reports on Land Tenure Surveys* for the various provinces published between 1967 and 1972.

—:Draft Policy of the Imperial Ethiopian Government of Agricultural Land Tenure, Mimeo, Addis Ababa, 1972.

PMAC: *Negarit Gazeta*. The major proclamations relating to land reform and agriculture are the following:

Proc. No. 31, April 1975 (Land distribution and rural organisations). No. 71, December 1975 (On peasant associations). No. 77, January 1976 as amended by No. 152, October 1978 (On agricultural taxes). No. 130, September 1977 (On formation of nation-wide peasant associations, AEPA). No. 138, March 1978 (Co-operative Societies). National Directive on Co-operatives of June 1979 (not published in the *Negarit Gazeta*). Proc. No. 223, May 1982 (On restructuring peasant associations).

WADU: *Agricultural Survey of Bolloso*, December 1971. WADI Publication No. 48. Wollaita-Soddo, 1976.

—:*1976 General Agricultural Survey Report.* WADU Publication No. 58. Wollaita-Soddo, 1976.

Unpublished Reports and Documents from the archives of Woreda administrations, Rural Development agencies, and Peasant Associations in the administrative districts in our study.

Various issues of the daily Amharic newspaper *Addis Zemen* for official statements, policy guide-lines, etc. pertaining to agriculture.

Books, Articles and Reports

Note: Ethiopian authors are listed alphabetically by first name.

M. Abdel-Fadil: *Development, Income Distribution and Social Change in Rural Egypt (1952—70). A Study in the Political Economy of Agrarian Transition.* London: Cambridge University Press, 1975.

Alula Abate and Tesfaye Teklu: Land Reform and Peasant Association in Ethiopia. A Case Study of Two Widely Differing Regions. Unpublished Paper, Institute of Development Research, Addis Ababa University, August 1978.

Befekadu Degefe: Economic Effects of Nationalisation-Distribution Policy. Unpublished manuscript, Faculty of Law, Addis Ababa University, June 1978.

L. Bondestam, 'Peoples and Capitalism in the North-eastern Lowlands of Ethiopia', *Journal of Modern African Studies,* vol. 12, no. 3, 1974.

J.W. Bruce: 'Ethiopia, Nationalisation of Rural Lands Proclamation.' Unpublished paper, University of Wisconsin Land Tenure Centre, Madison, Wisc, 1975.

C. Clapham: 'Centralisation and Local Response in Southern Ethiopia,' *African Affairs,* vol. 74, no. 294, 1975.

J.M. Coen et al.: *Revolution and Land Reform in Ethiopia.* Rural Development Occasional Paper No. 6. Cornell University, Ithaca, New York, 1976.

J.M. Cohen and P.H. Koehn: *Ethiopian Provincial and Municipal Government.* E. Lansing, Mich.: African Studies Centre, Michigan State University, 1980.

—:'Rural and Urban Land Reform in Ethiopia', *African Law Studies,* No. 14, 1977.

and D. Weintraub: *Land and Peasants in Imperial Ethiopia.* Assen: Van Gorcum, 1975.

Dessalegn Rahmato: Awassa, *A Limited Impact Study* (A Social Survey of a Provincial Town). IDR Research Report No. 29, Addis Ababa, December 1979.

—:'Conditions of the Ethiopian Peasantry', *Challenge,* vol. x, no. 2, 1970.

—:*Marx and Peasant Societies.* IDR Occasional Paper no. 15, Addis Ababa, January 1981.

Peter Dorner: *Land Reform and Economic Development.* Penguin Books, 1972.

G. Ellis: 'Land Tenancy Reform in Ethiopia, A Retrospective Analysis,' *Economic Development and Cultural Change,* vol. 28, no. 3, April 1980.

FAO: *Agriculture in Ethiopia* (Compiled by H.P. Huffnagel). Rome: FAO, 1961.

Fassil G. Kiros: 'Estimates of the Proportion of the Potential Work Year Allocated to Socio-Cultural Functions in Rural Ethiopia', *Ethiopian Journal of Development Research,* October 1976.

—:*An Investigation into the Problem of Fragmentation of Agricultural Land in Ethiopia in the Post-1975 Period.* IDR Research Report No. 31, Addis Ababa, June 1980.

Edmundo Flores: 'The Economics of Land Reform' in R. Stavenhagen (ed), *Agrarian Problems and Peasant Movements in Latin America.* Garden City: Anchor, 1970.

G. Galperin: 'Ethiopia: Stages of Agrarian Revolution,' *Asia and Africa Today* (Moscow), No. 6, 1981.

P. Gilkes: *The Dying Lion.* London: J. Friedmann, 1975.

F.V. Goricke: *Social and Political Factors Influencing the Application of Land Reform Measures in Ethiopia.* Saarbrucken: Verlag, 1979.

Henock Kifle: *Investigation on Mechanised Farming and Its Effects on Peasant Agriculture.* CADU Report No. 74, Assela, CADU 1974.

Allen Hoben: *Land Tenure Among the Amhara of Ethiopia.* Chicago: the University Press, 1975.

—:'Social Anthropology and Development Planning ... in Ethiopia,' *Journal of Modern African Studies,* vol. 10, no. 4, 1972.

—:Social Soundness of Agrarian Reform in Ethiopia. Unpublished Manuscript prepared for the U.S. AID Mission to Ethiopia, December 1976.

J. Holmberg: *Grain Marketing and Land Reform in Ethiopia.* Research Report No. 41. Uppsala: SIAS, 1977.

A. Hussain and K. Tribe: *Marxism and the Agrarian Question,* vol 2, *Russian Marxism and the Peasantry 1861—1930.* London: Macmillan Press, 1981.

G. Hyden: *Beyond Ujamaa in Tanzania.* Berkeley: Univ. of California Press, 1980.

I.L.O.: *Agrarian Reform with Particular Reference to Employment and Social Aspects.* Geneva: ILO, 1964.

Alain de Janvry: *The Agrarian Question and Reformism in Latin America.* Baltimore: Johns Hopkins Univ. Press. 1981.

Ingvar Jonsson: *Diffusion of Agricultural Innovations in Chillalo Awraja, Ethiopia.* IDR Research Report No. 17, Addis Ababa, June 1975.

J. Lawrence and H.S. Mann: 'FAO Land Policy Project,' *Ethiopia Observer,* vol. 9, no. 4, 1966.

D. Lehmann (ed.): *Agrarian Reform and Agrarian Reformism.* London: Faber and Faber, 1974.

D. Lehmann: 'The Death of Land Reform: A Polemic,' *World Development,* vol. 6, no. 3, 1978.

M. Lipton: 'Towards a Theory of Land Reform' in Lehmann (ed.).

K.J. Lundström: *North-Eastern Ethiopia: A Society in Famine.* Research Report No. 34, Uppsala: SIAS, 1976.

H.S. Mann: *Land Tenure in Chore (Shoa).* Addis Ababa: Institute of Ethiopian Studies, 1965.

J. Markakis: *Ethiopia: Anatomy of a Traditional Policy.* Oxford: Clarendon Press, 1974.

M. Ottaway 'Land Reform and Peasant Associations in Ethiopia', *Rural Africana,* Fall 1975.

T. Shanin (ed.): *Peasants and Peasant Societies:* Penguin Books, 1971.

Jack Shepherd: *The Politics of Starvation.* New York: Carnegie Endowment, 1975.

Michael Ståhl: *Contradictions in Agricultural Development. A Study of Three Minimum Package Projects in Southern Ethiopia.* Research Report No. 14, Uppsala: SIAS, 1973.

—: *Ethiopia: Political Contradictions in Agricultural Development.* Stockholm, 1974.

—: *New Seeds in Old Soil. A Study of the Land Reform Process in Western Wollega, Ethiopia 1975—76.* Research Report No. 40, Uppsala: SIAS, 1977.

R. Stavenhagen (ed.): See under Flores

Hung-Chao Tai: *Land Reform and Politics: A Comparative Analysis.* Berkeley: Univ. of California Press, 1974.

Tesfaye Teclu: *Socio-Economic Conditions in Shashemene 1978,—in Doddota 1978, ... in Dangla 1978.* IDR Research Report No. 26, 27, 28, Addis Ababa, 1979.

E.H. Tuma: *Twenty-Six Centuries of Agrarian Reform: A Comparative Analysis.* Berkeley: Univ. of California Press, 1965.

U.N. *Progress in Land Reform. Fourth Report.* New York: UN, 1966.

—: *Progress in Land Reform. Fifth Report.* New York UN, 1970.

L.J. Walinsky (ed.): *Agrarian Reform as Unfinished Business.* Oxford: Oxford University Press, 1977.

Doreen Warriner: *Land Reform in Principle and Practice.* Oxford: Clarendon Press, 1969.

E. Westphal: *Agricultural Systems in Ethiopia.* Wageningen: CAPD, 1975.

Eric Wolf: *Peasants.* Englewood Cliffs, N.J.: Prentice-Hall, 1966.

The Marxist Classics

K. Marx: 'Conspectus on Bakunin's *State and Anarchy*', in Saul K. Padover (ed.), *The Karl Marx Library,* vol. 3, *On the First International.* New York: McGraw-Hill, 1973.

—: 'The Nationalisation of the Land' in Marx and Engels, *Selected Works in Three Volumes,* vol. 2, Moscow: Progress Publishers, 1969.

F. Engels: 'The Peasant Question in France and Germany', ibid.

—: *The Peasant War in Germany,* 1870 edn. New York: International Publishers, 1966.

V.I. Lenin: *The Development of Capitalism in Russia,* 1907 edn. Moscow: Progress Publishers, 1964.

—: *Selected Works in Three Volumes,* New York: International Publishers, 1967.

Journals

The Journal of Peasant Studies: various issues.